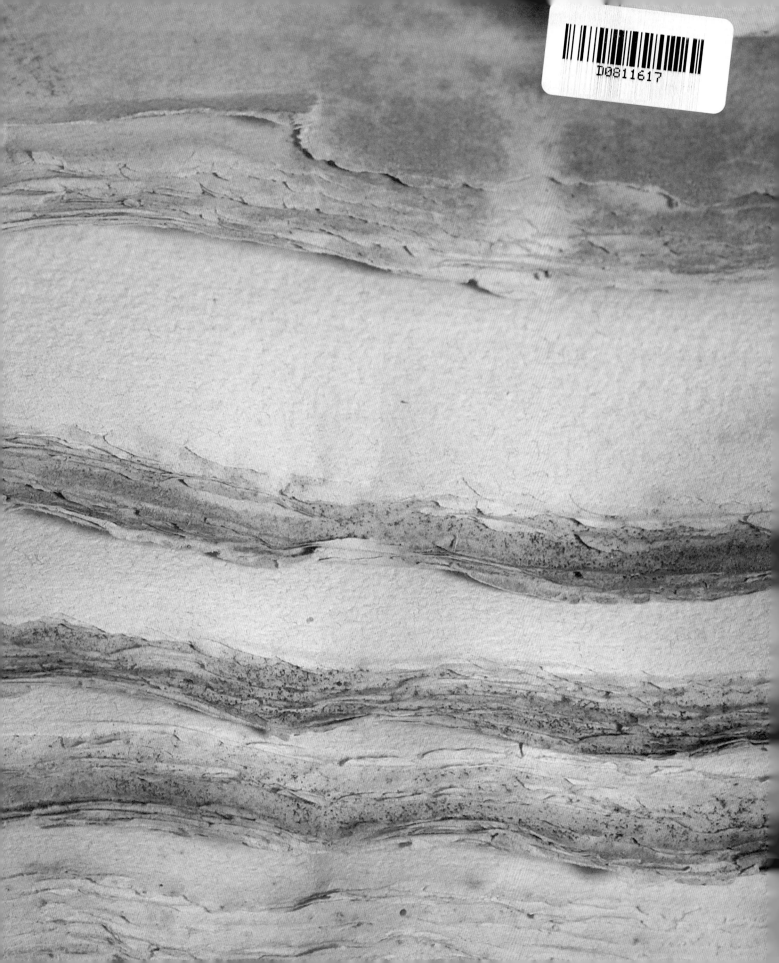

Essentially
FRENCH

Essentially FRENCH

HOMES WITH CLASSIC FRENCH STYLE

JOSEPHINE RYAN

PHOTOGRAPHY BY CLAIRE RICHARDSON

RYLAND PETERS & SMALL
LONDON • NEW YORK

'If I were asked to say what is at once the most important production of Art and the thing most to be longed for, I should answer, a beautiful House.'

WILLIAM MORRIS

SENIOR DESIGNER Megan Smith
COMMISSIONING EDITOR Annabel Morgan
LOCATION RESEARCH Josephine Ryan
and Jess Walton
CONTRIBUTING EDITOR Helen Ridge
PRODUCTION MANAGER Gordana Simakovic
ART DIRECTOR Leslie Harrington
PUBLISHING DIRECTOR Alison Starling

First published in 2009
This revised edition published in 2018 by
Ryland Peters and Small
20–21 Jockey's Fields
London WC1R 4BW
and
341 East 116th Street
New York, NY 10029
www.rylandpeters.com

10 9 8 7 6 5 4 3 2 1

Text © Josephine Ryan 2009, 2018
Design and photographs
© Ryland Peters & Small 2009, 2018

ISBN: 978-1-78879-024-6

A CIP record for this book is
available from the British Library.

Library of Congress Cataloging-in-Publication
Data for the original edition of this book is as
follows:

Ryan, Josephine.
    Essentially French : homes with classic
French style / Josephine Ryan ;
photography by Claire Richardson. --1st ed.

        p. cm.
    Includes index.
    ISBN 978-1-84597-906-5
    1. Interior decoration. 2. Antiques in
interior decoration--France. 3. Antique
dealers--Homes and haunts. I. Richardson,
Claire, 1969- II. Title.
    NK2115.5.A5R93 2009
    747--dc22

                    2009017148
Printed and bound in China

INTRODUCTION

Essentially French offers a privileged glimpse into the homes of a select few antiques dealers – those who share my lifelong love for France and for French antiques. For this book, this select band generously opened the doors to their homes – idiosyncratic private spaces that showcase the passions of their owners. In a world where the relentless conveyer belt of mass production strives to meet a seemingly insatiable demand for the new, some of us still have a genuine regard for and deep-seated delight in the craftsmanship of the past. The antiques dealers whose homes are featured in this book are all members of this tribe – a tribe I have affectionately christened 'The Last Gypsies'.

I love my job. I have been an antiques dealer for close to 20 years now, and I still look forward to getting up in the morning for work. In truth, it is less a job and more a passion; a way of life that I count myself fortunate to make a living from. I still love the early winter mornings; buying by torchlight, wrapped up so tightly you can barely see what you're buying or who you're buying from. Then there are the even earlier summer mornings, seeing a glorious sunrise over a racecourse while uncovering someone else's discarded treasures. Later, there's the inevitable gathering around the coffee bar, comparing bargains (or the lack of them). I revel in coming back to my shop and unwrapping layers of old newspaper and used bubble wrap to reveal sundry disparate objects that, when arranged, will create a beautiful still life in the shop... until they find a new home for the next chapter of their lives.

I find buying abroad a huge thrill. Some may think it a busman's holiday, but the thrill of the chase can be even stronger on foreign turf. Language differences are no barrier to the diehard dealer – we are united by a common spirit the world over. Then there's the heady hit of buying at auction, never knowing if you're going to win your lot, struggling to resist the buzz of breaking your self-imposed price barrier. And the in-house trading! If a boatload of antiques dealers were washed up on a desert island, they would quickly establish a brisk micro-economy selling crabs and coconuts to the highest bidder, each of us in line, believing he or she can get a better price than the last!

The homes featured in this book are every bit as varied and as interesting as their idiosyncratic owners. Among others, there are two stylish Londoners whose home reveals a fascination not only with France but also with 18th-century Sweden, a Sussex couple whose home will make you SMILE and a handsome rogue from Provence with a penchant for quirky fairground art. The one thing the dealers all have in common is, of course, an unquenchable passion for the *object trouvé*. It's a passion that even surpasses the need for profit... although a bit of extra cash also has an undeniable allure!

There are many treasures within these pages, varying from a Queen Anne inlaid commode to a worthless fragment of a Parisian zinc rooftop. What links these objects is the fact that each and every piece forms part of a harmonious whole – a whole that each dealer creates with his or her own particular eye.

If beauty is in the eye of the beholder, then I hope that you will behold these pages and enjoy. And, if you are inspired to start collecting yourself, rejoice, because many of the owners of these houses have shops, so you will be able to inspect, appreciate and perhaps even carry home some of their wares.

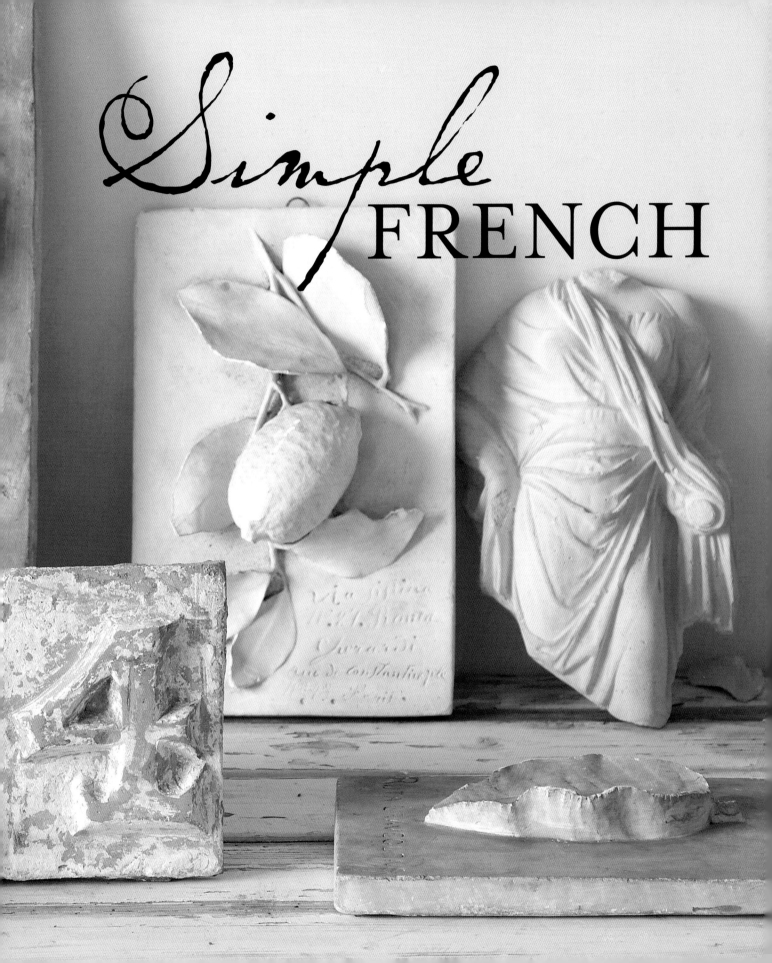

Simple FRENCH

Brought up in south-west Ireland with parents who loved to trawl junk shops and the auction houses, I had an appreciation of objets d'art from a very early age. With roots in France on my mother's side, I also had a fascination for all things French.

A RUSTIC IDYLL

Someone once told me 'Better to be born lucky than rich'. I consider myself to be the former. Nothing predestined me for my 'profession' of antiques dealing. Indeed, it is not so much a profession as a vocation.

I could never have envisaged where my initial foray into the life of dealing was to lead. Sixteen years ago, starting off with a pair of bronze candlesticks, an old wooden toilet seat and other pieces surplus to requirements, I borrowed a friend's red van and trundled off in the early hours to flog my goods at England's largest trade fair in Newark, Lincolnshire. Perhaps it was beginner's luck, but I sold everything, then immediately went out and spent the proceeds on more stock. Like all gamblers, I was hooked.

Now I have a shop that's fully stocked as well as a London home full of treasures I can't bear to part with, and I am starting to collect more beautiful things to furnish my latest acquisition – the most beautiful house in the South of France (in my opinion!). I first visited the town of Uzès in the Gard region of France about eight years ago. The Gard was once part of Provence, and the region has the same charm and beauty as that area, but without the glitz. The Gardois are rural folk who work the land. Every season yields an

ABOVE *Old glazed terracotta cheese moulds are now used to house and display a collection of antique silver knives, pewter spoons and 1980s Habitat wooden-handled everyday cutlery.* ABOVE RIGHT *Sunflowers picked from the field next door reflect the large contemporary oil painting of my favourite flowers that is propped against the kitchen wall.* OPPOSITE *The kitchen is in the original cellar or* cave, *which would have once been home to the farm animals. The old Spanish trestle table is draped with an antique linen runner.*

abundance of sumptuous produce: artichokes and asparagus in spring, plump and lush apricots and peaches in summer, figs and, of course, every variety of grape in the autumn months.

When hunting for my new home, I looked at more houses than I care to remember. And I never experienced that instinctive '*that's* the one I want' feeling until I walked through the rather grandiose gates of the property I now own. To borrow a French phrase, this house was truly *dans son jus* – in other words, it hadn't been repaired, painted or polished. Nowadays, this is a quality that's increasingly hard to find, with so many houses having been tinkered around with and 'improved'.

But this house was definitely 'in its own juice'. In a deep valley, with no mobile phone reception,

LEFT *The ground-floor salon leads into the kitchen. This low-beamed room is warm in winter, when I have huge log fires blazing, and cool and refreshing in summer. The furniture is an eclectic mix of styles: a modern leather sofa, a wing-back chair covered in antique French linen and an armchair awaiting recovering, draped with a Moroccan throw.* **ABOVE** *A collection of intricately carved treen objects and a tiny toy rabbit.*

stands an ancient stone hamlet of 11 houses that all touch each other at some point. Mine has a single cypress tree, which towers above the rooftops and is something of a landmark. There is no boulangerie, bar or tabac. The only sounds are the hum of the crickets and the combined cacophony of frogs croaking, donkeys braying and goats bleating. This is *Jean de Florette* country (part of the film was, in fact, shot in the Place aux Herbes in Uzès). Here, water is a precious commodity – the heat of the summer sizzles the tarmac, while in the winter the smell of woodsmoke from the chimneys is evocative of another age.

This *mas* had been standing empty for 16 long years. The previous owner was a potter, and I felt the fact that her kiln and wheel were left behind could only be a good omen. Making pots was one of my very first artistic endeavours, and something I have always hoped to return to.

The house is not easy to navigate, and it took several tours before I could orientate myself. Four different staircases lead to the upper level. Rooms lead off each other, and there are terraces and corners at every turn, four functioning fireplaces and a kitchen with no running water. Though cold and dusty and festooned with cobwebs, the house

OPPOSITE *The mantelpiece in the main salon is home to an intriguing still life. The objects displayed include a tangle of glass dolls' eyes and an African iron bird, which would have been used as a form of currency, both set in front of an 18th-century map of France.* ABOVE *This useful console provides decorative storage in the second salon. On display are various frames, a rack of test tubes, a birdcage, a moody landscape and piles of textiles. The unusual folding bistro chair was found in the nearby town of Barjac.* RIGHT *A detail of the irresistible collection of vivid silk threads.*

THIS PAGE *The only adornment in this sparse, calm bedroom is a moody painting by an Australian artist of a naked woman embracing a lizard. The floor is pressed, painted concrete, incised with a design of octagonal motifs arranged in a formal grid.*
OPPOSITE *The main bathroom overlooks the surrounding countryside, the constant natural light making bathing a sublime experience. The unusual large basin, one of the only original fittings left in the house, is in immaculate condition with porcelain taps. A small double-sided magnifying mirror hanging from the wall and a branch from a Judas tree in an IKEA vase encourage a bright white smile.*
OPPOSITE BELOW *An exceptional 19th-century French silver gilt bistro mirror reflects the view of the hills beyond.*

was not damp, and the original terracotta roof tiles were firmly intact with no signs of leakage.

The house sang out to me. The utility room, with a gnarled old door and a beautiful oversized iron key, housed a vast Heath-Robinson-like boiler, which, miraculously, proved to function well with only a little attention. The maker's mark on this monolith was Le Mercier: my mother's maiden name. She was the one who told me it was better to be born lucky. Well… mothers are always right! I had found my French home.

When decorating, my brief to myself was to create something quite different to my house in London. My vision was both rustic and modern, comfortable and relaxed, combining splashes of

colour with a leaning towards Morocco. It is difficult to describe the floor plan, as one can start from several points. The *cave* that is now the kitchen originally housed animals, and parts of the house date back to as early as 1700. The original terracotta floor tiles in the living room are pitted and polished – evidence of decades upon decades of footfall. The scale of the rooms and overall feel of the house suggest this was not an agricultural worker's abode, but that of a landowner. The enormous, ornate iron gates were certainly installed by an owner of some means.

My first summer here I described as 'glamping'. The kitchen hadn't been refurbished and the nearest water source was a tap in the courtyard. The lap pool I dream of is in the distant future. But I have already made my mark. The thick walls needed little more than a brush down, and the windows a good clean. French bistro chairs are used inside and out, bought mostly at local *puces* or *brocantes* and always in need of a little TLC. An ex-display cream leather sofa from The Conran Shop provides comfort and contrast. Pieces of furniture bought years before with my French house in mind, and stashed in the barns of various friends ever since, have finally found their resting place.

Every thing I possess has a peculiar charm of its own. I often choose a piece of porcelain with a chip or a crack, rather than one that's perfect. In my view, it's the imperfections that make life more interesting. Some pieces will stay here, others will find their way back to my shop in London for someone else to own so that they can enjoy a little of the French dream. And when I sit in the garden on the stone bench under my very own fig tree, I feel lucky… very, very lucky.

ABOVE *The unusual high-backed chair — the most comfortable in the house for playing chess — has been christened the 'Cahal Chair' (my son has taken it for his own). Among the items displayed on the battered and rusty bistro table are a toy donkey, an African iron sculpture and a chunky modern glass vase with a branch from the fig tree that grows in the garden.*

RIGHT *The original kitchen, now a study, has an enormous fireplace once used for cooking. Now it's the focal point of this room with a view. An 18th-century Carmargue bottle, an English studio piece c. 1960 and a small French carafe are grouped to one side.*

BELOW *The main bedroom is large and high-ceilinged, so the modern four-poster is not overwhelming. Here, too, nature has been brought inside, in the shape of a huge olive branch acting as a unique chandelier.*

ABOVE *Leading off the master bedroom is the terrace, with uninterrupted views across the valley. The driftwood bench is a dreamy seat of repose.* **LEFT** *A collection of large, smooth rocks from the nearby fast-flowing river at Collias.* **OPPOSITE** *In the shade of an enormous fig tree, a French iron weathervane oversees the courtyard (above left). Wild at heart; a lover's bouquet in front of the ancient door with its original iron key (above right). A collection of* **petits pots** *used for shots of coffee taken on the terrace (below left). Fresh almonds are soft, furry and pearly white, and delicious with a glass of local Viognier (below right).*

Between the ancient towns of Montpellier and Nîmes in southern France lies a tiny picturesque village. It is here that the renowned antiques dealer Appley Hoare and her daughter Zoë have transformed a ruined limestone **bastide** into a serene and beautiful home.

ALL SERENE

It was many years earlier when living in Sydney, Australia, that Appley Hoare's love affair with the antiques business first began. Working as a stylist, she inevitably came into close contact with those in the trade and soon realized that she wanted to be part of that world. Appley became a force to be reckoned with, and she spent many years shipping antique furniture from France back to Australia. Then in the mid-1990s she moved to London, bringing her very individual style to Belgravia's Pimlico Road, where she and Zoë set up their antiques business selling all things French, large, rustic and beautiful.

Appley and Zoë first stumbled across and fell in love with this picturesque village while on a buying trip and staying in a very beautiful *chambre d'hote* in the village. As their visits became increasingly frequent, Appley ended up buying the derelict *bastide* (grand farmhouse) next door. The homes of dealers inevitably mirror the stock of their shops, and Appley's home in France is no exception.

OPPOSITE *Appley builds up impressive collections of plaster mouldings, fragments and columns, then sells virtually everything and starts collecting all over again. A few pieces, however — old favourites and gifts with sentimental value — are always kept back.* **ABOVE RIGHT** *This moody little oil of a bath recreates the charming guest room with its own bathing area.* **RIGHT** *The memory of a very special man lives on in this musical sculpture — a quirky mounting of a battered old bugle.*

TOP LEFT *The initials on these ironed and starched linen napkins do not belong to any of the members of this household.* BELOW LEFT *Local wine seems to taste so much better when drunk from thick-rimmed, antique glass rummers.* BOTTOM LEFT *It's impressive to own such a large quantity of original china in such good condition. These 19th-century Gien blue and white plates are ready for service* tout de suite. BELOW *The functioning side of this kitchen is evidence of how well the ancient and modern have come together. The open concrete shelves have a Moroccan feel, and baskets are used for storage.* OPPOSITE *In the kitchen, the long zinc-topped table, formally set, awaits eight lucky guests.*

ABOVE *Despite its soaring height, the salon is serene and comfortable. Dried hydrangeas in the 18th-century stone fireplace mimic the soft stone palette of the* objets, *furniture and soft furnishings.* **LEFT** *The latest plaster addition — a love gift never to be parted with.* **OPPOSITE ABOVE** *'A' is for antique, acquisitive and animated. And here, on the mantelpiece in the salon, 'A' is also for Appley.* **OPPOSITE BELOW** *A home without books is like an empty decanter. Although purely decorative, the books surely contain words of wisdom, and no doubt the honey-coloured wine is delicious.*

The renovation of the farmhouse was a massive
project, which predictably went well over budget
and took much longer than expected to complete.
But it was well worth the wait. The end result is
a unique modern interior in an 18th-century
building – vast but not overwhelming, comfortable
but not in the least twee and as tranquil and
uplifting as a cathedral.

The modest gate to the property gives no
indication of what lies beyond. With uninterrupted
views over the surrounding countryside, the
formal landscaped garden is made up of one
gigantic bed densely planted with no less than

60 large balls of lavender. A decorative white-painted iron gate leads to the swimming pool and pool house. Close to the house, in the shade of one of four mature olive trees and in front of the cypresses flanking the front door, are two separate outdoor dining areas. The traditional bistro tables and chairs are typical of those that Appley is famous for selling at her London shop.

A modern glazed iron door – in stark contrast to the surrounding limestone, which is the inspiration behind the palette of colours used inside – opens straight onto the kitchen. The floor is poured and polished concrete, as are all the floors on this level, while the walls are off-white unpainted plaster. The focal point is the early

OPPOSITE FAR LEFT *These 19th-century Swiss violin parts, artfully displayed in Zoë's bedroom, play a quiet tune.* OPPOSITE BELOW *The 18th-century French painted armoire in Appley's bedroom holds a collection of linens.* OPPOSITE RIGHT *Another 18th-century armoire in the living room is home to paisley and velvet cushions.* RIGHT *On the bistro table in the guest bedroom, the letter 'A' — a recurrent motif in this house — stands on this occasion for asleep.* BELOW *This slipper bath occupies a corner of the bedroom.*

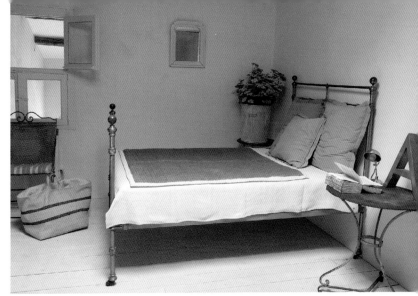

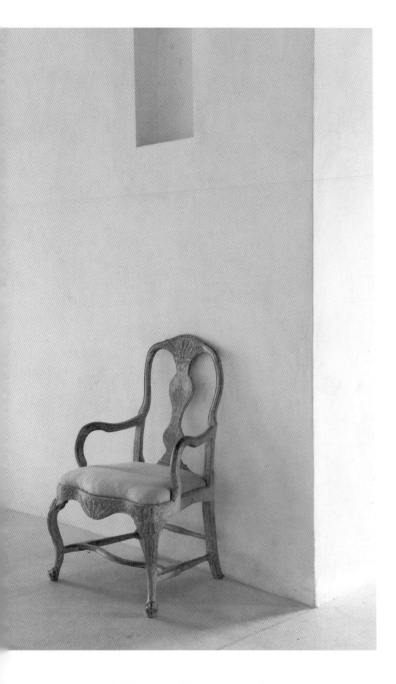

RIGHT *These 19th-century fireman's ladders in their original burned red paint are five metres tall.*
OPPOSITE *In the eaves, this workroom, with a French work table showing remnants of original paint and a nursing chair, both 19th century, allows space for creative expression. The room also holds extra beds, for when there are more guests than beds elsewhere.*

19th-century French, zinc-covered dining table surrounded with classic metal Tolix chairs. Equally impressive is the enormous marble-topped dresser base, with a bespoke wooden plate rack on top housing a striking collection of 19th-century blue and white Gien plates. The kitchen units, if you can call them that, were made by a Moroccan artisan and give the kitchen a very individual 'unfitted' look. Despite its size, the room lends itself to both informal lunches for two and elegant dinners for large numbers.

The passage from room to room flows easily. While the rooms are clearly individual, there is a feeling of continuity between them. The kitchen leads to the vast salon with its comfortable, oversized Conran sofas covered in neutral linens. Here, the back wall is half exposed limestone, half off-white plaster, and fitted with an 18th-century French stone fireplace that was found in Spain and added during restoration. Displayed on the mantelpiece is a collection of Appley's finds,

ABOVE *Without the subtle, square recess, this corner of the soaring space at the heart of the house would be just a blank and featureless expanse of wall, but the inclusion of the shallow* niche *transforms it into a concrete installation that cannot be moved, bought or sold. The 18th-century Swedish chair is pure and perfect in its simplicity, and is not for sale either.*

ABOVE *One of the outdoor dining areas, with seating for two in the shade of gnarled olive trees.* **FAR LEFT** *The French doors in the grand salon open onto an enormous balcony with extensive views over the surrounding countryside.* **LEFT** *This unusual iron gate, with its bullrush and flower motifs, leads to the swimming pool.* **OPPOSITE** *Sitting at the old bistro table for a mid-morning read and a glass of pastis is about as French as you can get. The four carvers, with their original turquoise paint, echo the aqua tones of the water in the pool behind.*

including a tin letter 'A', a miniature mannequin and a 1920s grotesque. The coffee table is a large piece of scagliola atop four 19th-century finials originally from a bridge in Scotland.

Parallel to the kitchen and behind the salon is an enormous space that can be viewed as the nave of this cathedral-like home. The original beams, now fitted with theatre lights, are still in place. The furnishings are chic, beautiful and sparse, with each object speaking for itself, but they are also transient, depending on what Appley needs in the London shop. At the moment, two red, five-metres-high, 19th-century wooden fireman's ladders from Lyon are propped against one wall, while a 1960s plaster-cast of the Louvre's *Venus de Milo* looms large in the corner by the window, but any day now they could be on their way to be sold.

There are two huge bedrooms with their own generous bathrooms on this floor. Similar in style, they are also spacious enough to have their own individual seating areas. Appley's room is decorated with antique French textiles and linens in a palette of hues ranging from natural creams to bold reds and the odd deep purple. She is as passionate about textiles as she is about furniture, to the extent that an 18th-century armoire is used to store the surplus.

A freestanding staircase built from concrete leads to the second floor. Here, the rooms are on a smaller scale, but retain the simple elegance of those downstairs. Throughout, the flooring is painted wooden scaffolding boards. The intimate guest bedroom is simply furnished with an iron bed and antique indigo-dyed linen, with a slipper bath in the corner. The room conveys an air of utter peace and tranquillity.

During renovation, Appley did little to the exterior of the *bastide* except sympathetic repairs, but the dilapidated interior has been transformed into a simple yet charismatic home. Her clever combination of the old with the new, with a strong Gallic sensibility, is nothing less than a huge success story, just like her antiques business.

For Victoria Davar, antiques dealing is in her bones: both her father and grandmother before her were dealers of great repute. She and her partner Shane Meredith are very much part of the new generation of antiques dealers — they may deal in all things old, but they are entirely modern.

SLIGHTLY FOXED

Victoria Davar and Shane Meredith are appreciative of all aspects of the arts and broadly knowledgeable about everything from 1950s British ceramics to 18th-century Swedish furniture. Both own long-established shops on south-west London's vibrant Lillie Road: a street of very individual antiques shops that has witnessed many changes over the years, but that steadfastly defies the insidious encroachment of the high street and the invasion of bland chains. Victoria and Shane once owned homes on opposite sides of London, but two years ago they decided to throw their lot in together and give their two brindle Staffordshire Bull Terrier cross-breeds a stable home.

Leafy London streets can all look the same to the untrained eye, with a jumble of housing stock that varies from Georgian townhouses and Victorian terraces to Deco-style 1930s semis and 1950s post-war infills. Victoria and Shane's house, built around 1840, sits on one such street, and boasts both duchesses and dustmen

RIGHT *The basement kitchen is home to a harmonious mix of Gallic and Scandinavian pieces. The many mirrors create a web of magical reflections. There are Venetian wall sconces, a French overmantel, two convexes (one seen in reflection), a pair of mirrored doors and, centre stage on the Swedish drop-leaf table, a fine rectangular mirror plate.*

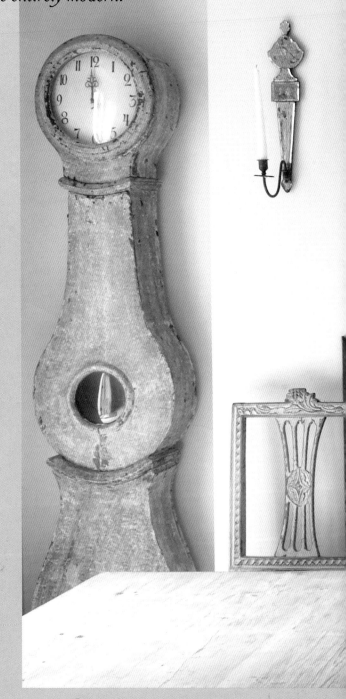

OPPOSITE *The camaraderie of antiques dealers is evident in the presence of one of Katharine Pole's distinctive cushions, which she makes from fabrics from the 18th to mid-20th century. The early 18th-century carved phoenix sits on a mirrored 1930s Italian coffee table.* **ABOVE AND CENTRE** *Nine oil paintings of popes in their original frames gaze approvingly upon an early 18th-century carved Madonna without Child!* **ABOVE RIGHT** *Vicky's collection of mercury glass balls remind her of the magic of childhood German Christmases.*

as neighbours. When they bought the house, a good omen seemed to signal that the move was meant to be. On receipt of the keys, they were also handed a creased brown envelope containing all the deeds of ownership since the house was built – true works of art, bearing their original ruby red wax seals and the exquisite penmanship of previous owners and lawyers long since forgotten.

The eternal search for undiscovered treasure is the antiques dealer's *raison d'etre*. The crumbling blue paintwork of Victoria and Shane's home

conceals a jewel box of delights. Their house holds the cream of the crop, a wealth of exquisite pieces that fall into a category Shane describes as 'keepers'. Keepers are those special pieces that dealers stumble across on a buying trip, but just can't bear to sell on; those objects with an undefinable quality that call out to you, whether they be large or small, wildly expensive or a complete bargain – a teddy bear with one ear, perhaps, a table with an oh-so-elegant turn to its legs or a helmet with your initials on it. These

'keepers' become treasured possessions and lifelong companions; the components that come together to make a unique and beautiful home.

It's inspiring and instructive to see how Victoria and Shane have chosen to display and arrange their acquisitions and treasures. Despite its exquisite contents, their house is no museum, but a much-loved home furnished with the perfect mix of important pieces, personal items and mementoes, and pieces of modern art (Victoria's sister is a celebrated artist based in Cologne), as well as all the usual ephemera of daily life. A house can be compared to a chessboard and the furniture

OPPOSITE ABOVE *Vicky admits that this 18th–century Italian mirror is the most expensive thing she has ever bought. She acquired it in Toulouse, but it was originally from a château near Paris.* **OPPOSITE BELOW** *A miniature galleon–shaped French crystal chandelier has the spirit of the story of Peter Pan.* **ABOVE** *In the bedroom, a pair of English 1920s unicorn heads takes pride of place on a French table with cabriole legs. A year of dry–scraping revealed the original white paint. This is Vicky's favourite piece of furniture in the house.* **RIGHT** *The bathroom boasts an important oil of three nudes. A 19th–century Italian silver gilt candlestick affords romantic bathing.*

to the pieces, each one having its own rightful place on the board. As with a game of chess, when it comes to arranging furniture, the skill lies in knowing the right moves. A talent for harmonious arrangement can perhaps be learned, but the skill does rely on having a good eye, appreciating pieces for their beauty (rather than value), being unafraid of mixing eras and styles, understanding colour and light and, most importantly, having confidence in your own vision.

Victoria and Shane were lucky enough to begin with a structurally sound building. The house didn't need total refurbishment, just repainting from top to toe. They chose subtle and elegant tones, painting ceilings, walls and woodwork in the same colour throughout, creating a seamless backdrop for their treasures. It's a very grown-up look that enhances and enlarges the space.

The living room, situated on the first floor, manages to be both grand and simple, comfortable and welcoming. The slightly oversized furniture provides a subtle Alice-in-Wonderland effect, while the light streaming in at the large, original sash windows contributes to the feeling of calm well-being. The walls are home to an impressive collection of antique mirrors. The smoky, atmospheric glass of these foxed looking glasses

ABOVE LEFT *The subtle colours of this garlic plait make it worthy of display alongside a treasured 'love gift' — a defunct but charming old thermometer and a tiny foxed mirror in an exquisite silver gilt frame.*

LEFT *Two tiny jelly moulds and an even tinier silver spoon have been given a new life as salt cellars. Using objects for something other than their original purpose brings quirkiness and originality to any kitchen.*

makes them works of art in their own right, the gradual process of mercurial decay being impossible to imitate. Each and every one, from the tiniest convex to the grandest gilt pier glass, has its own entirely unique patination.

Even on a dull day, the basement kitchen doesn't feel dark or dreary. It possesses the same panache as the rest of the house. Here, the functional and decorative sit side by side. But nothing is selected in a spirit of utility alone – every item was chosen for its beauty of form, ensuring that a feeling of elegance prevails. Upstairs, the master bedroom is simply and sparsely furnished with more oversized pieces, creating a calm and intimate effect. Next door, the guest room introduces a splash of brightness to the otherwise subtle palette.

One feels that in this elegant townhouse the 'keepers' are here to stay, as are their owners and their collections – the wing-back armchairs, silver mercury balls, crumbling statuary and the canines – what lucky Staffies they are!

BELOW *The kitchen is the perfect blend of the old and the new. Three old wooden signs are used as artworks, IKEA units are coupled with chunky, worn breadboards and a floating shelf shows off an impressive collection of white and cream plates, bowls, tureens and pots.*

ABOVE LEFT, CENTRE AND LEFT *Shane's shoes, Vicky's dogs, a naked lady, a cat, a lamb and a handbag!* ABOVE *This monochrome portrait c. 1920, with a face reminiscent of Frida Kahlo's work, is by the artist C. Perilhou who worked just outside Uzès. The unusual lampshade of a map of Paris was bought from one of a band of male dealers affectionately nicknamed Les 3 Graces.*

THIS PAGE *The guest bedroom welcomes ailing friends in their hour of need. The oversized 19th-century French wing–back armchair, with huge 'ears' like a teddy bear's, was an invalid's chair.*

Carved wooden gates with flaky powder-blue paint guard the entrance to Stéphane Broutin's home. Originally from India, they are a beautiful anomaly in the town of L'Isle sur la Sorgue.

THE LION'S DEN

The gates open onto a high-vaulted, wide stone corridor. Some would use this space for parking, but Stéphane, like all antiques dealers, has a huge regard for the past and would not want to crush the ghosts of the cavalry that passed through many years ago. Today, almost as a homage to those horses, a life-size, carved and painted wooden donkey, originally from a fairground, nods its articulated head in welcome to visiting civilians.

LEFT *These typically French terracotta vessels create a striking still life in the dining room. Such everyday objects inspired artists as great as Cézanne to create works of art that depicted the ordinary as beautiful.*
BELOW *Originally from a fairground, this life-size carved and painted donkey with an articulated head stands at the entrance to the house.*

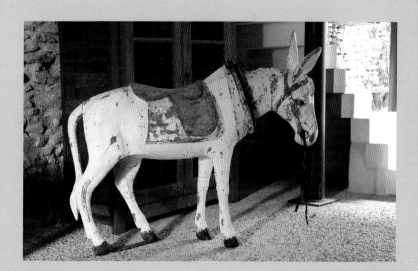

Back in the Middle Ages, this extraordinary house was created essentially out of the rear of this corridor. When Stéphane bought it in 2004, it was a virtual ruin, and it took him three painstaking, meticulous years to restore it to its present glory. Today, beyond the wooden gates, modern glazed iron doors lead into a continuous space containing the dining and kitchen areas. Identical doors at the far end open onto a tiny courtyard, with the perpetual trickling of water from a fountain.

The kitchen unit on one side is an old boulangerie shop fitting, beautifully fit for its new purpose, with ultra-modern fittings and black stone surfaces – perfect for pastry rolling. The off-white polished concrete floors have a dull sheen and are a joy to walk on with their under-floor heating. The dining area is colourful but not garish, and a fabulous collection of pillar-box red metal chairs sits around one of the chunky wooden tables that Stéphane is famous for.

Even though the house is not blessed with an abundance of natural light, it doesn't feel gloomy. The salon is probably the darkest room, but Stéphane has worked with, not against, the lack of light to create a womb-like, comfortable den. All the furniture and fittings are large and dark. Presiding over everything, above the fireplace, is the only permanent female present, and a very important one at that – the Madonna (and Child).

While his eye is naturally drawn to the slightly shabby and distressed, Stéphane is an absolute perfectionist – in his previous life he was a pastry chef, so precision comes naturally. But though pristine and immaculate, this is most definitely a man's house. The masculine collection of lions in all guises, from bronze sculptures, oversized plaster heads and oil paintings on canvas to a disparate display of the creatures on the salon table, reveal that the owner is a confident Leo. A handsome, bohemian rogue, Stéphane lives in

ABOVE LEFT *No self-respecting chef would be without a fine collection of knives, and you would expect an antiques dealer to have steel blades with olive wood handles. Here is the ultimate collection for finely slicing the best carpaccio.* **ABOVE RIGHT** *The large, glazed-front dresser has no back, allowing the beauty of the stone walls to show through the neatly stacked rows of the ubiquitous French bistro glass.*

the house alone, while his wife lives in her house up the road – a recipe for a successful marriage, where one's own creativity remains uncompromised!

Going up to the mezzanine floor to Stéphane's study, the house begins to feel almost warren-like. The sparsely furnished study has just a white 1960s lacquered wood desk with little on it and a shelf unit from a boulangerie spanning one wall. Floating upwards from the study to the master bedroom and bathroom is the cast-stone, freestanding staircase – an architectural joy.

The master bedroom is large enough to have its own seating area – the 1970s sofa, chair and stool are upholstered in a tweedy, sandy-hued fabric, reminiscent of the desert depicted in the modern painting and the Philippe Starck faux cacti. The

LEFT *The minimalist purity of this exquisitely constructed stone staircase would surely gain John Pawson's seal of approval. The metal ram, a piece of art by a local artist, baas in wholehearted agreement.*

ABOVE *The 19th-century bull's head, no doubt from a boucherie, looks as if it is ready to stampede free from the industrial extractor fan. The 19th-century enamel sign serves as an original oven splashback.*

almost wall-to-wall and floor-to-ceiling bespoke wardrobe has stripped pine doors, and there's just enough space above for a wonderful old shop sign: '*Antiquités*', lest Stéphane should forget, one hazy morning, what his job is. Also on this floor, overlooking the sleepy street, an indoor, Moroccan-inspired terrace has its own mini kitchen for lazy morning coffees and late-night snifters.

It is always refreshing to come across a home as original as this one. Entirely confident in conception and detail, with no attempt to plagiarize or copy, this home is as unique as every item in it. As with antiques dealers worldwide, you will find the best of the stock not in Stéphane's shop but at home, kept away from customers' eagerly signed cheques. Every job has its perks, and this is a pretty good one.

LEFT *Why clean out the ashes when the flames from last night's fire have burned out? The smouldering embers leave an aroma with traces of a distant romantic age that no scented candle can hope to emulate. The 19th-century French fireplace is stone.*
ABOVE *This ancient beam is host to a bundle of mistletoe. One wonders how many embraces these rooms have witnessed.*

ABOVE LEFT *The stone staircase to the study is home to an exquisitely carved Italian figure, triumphant upon her bow-fronted Swedish corner cupboard.* ABOVE RIGHT *A pride of lions in many mediums.* BELOW *Majestic but fragile, this plaster bull surveys the scene from a chest of drawers with unusual rounded corners.* OPPOSITE *Philippe Starck faux cacti set the scene in the main bedroom. The painting is mesmerizing—you almost feel you're in the front seat of a convertible Chevy, the wind in your hair, speeding through the Arizona desert.*

The shop is also in Sorgue, and Stéphane can walk to work in two minutes. His taste for the big and the bold, so evident in his home, means that there are no dainty porcelain pieces for sale here. Expect, instead, enormous five-metre-long gnarled tables with legs like tree trunks, paint-spattered like a Pollock painting, and other such gargantuan pieces of furniture.

When not in his shop, Stéphane is on the road, driving across France, in far-flung corners of Italy and as far away as Sweden, in pursuit of the largest, the most unusual and the best. Anyone wishing to furnish a château should look no further. But get in there quickly, before he takes off with the lion's share of his finds.

LEFT *Stéphane's collection of enamel signs continues in his dark masculine bathroom.* **ABOVE** *Reclaimed pine doors have been used to build a fitted wardrobe, home to a collection of antique linen sheets.*

BELOW *The guest bedroom has a touch of The Emperor's New Clothes. Not for the vain, this frame without a looking glass is a surreal tease. The large drill bit in the corner becomes a piece of modern art.*

ABOVE *A 19th-century barn door has been turned on its side and reincarnated as an unusual bedhead.*
FAR LEFT *The comfortable leather club armchair on the interior terrace has a view over the streets of Sorgue.*
LEFT *In the bedroom, these dried hydrangea heads echo the moody blues and pinks in the Hopperesque landscape behind.*

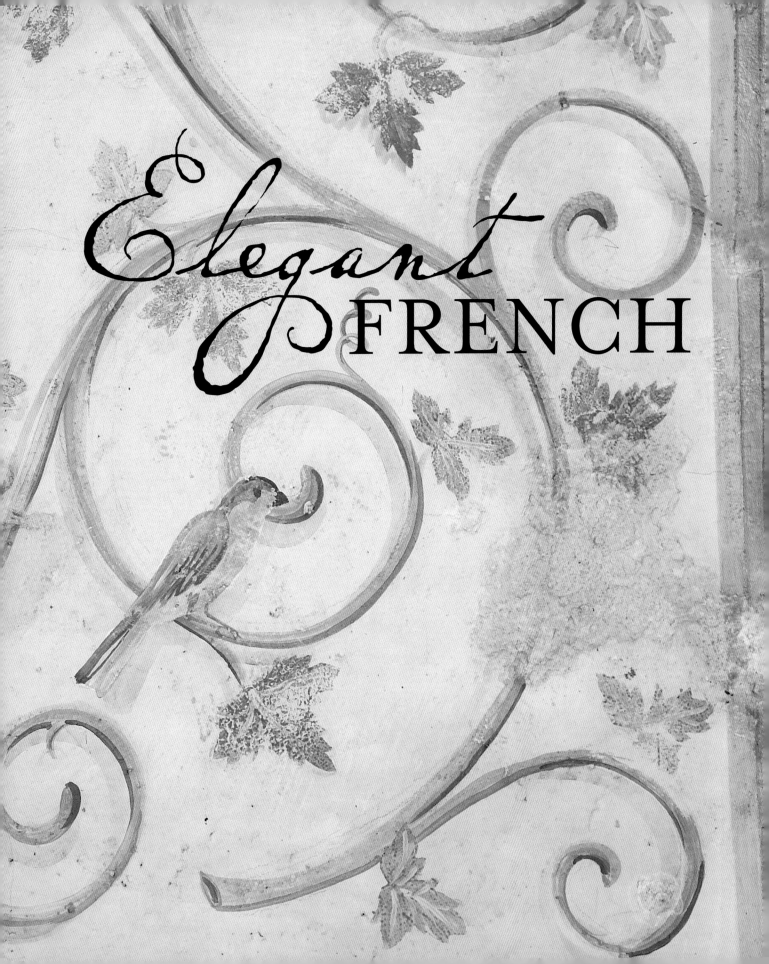

Elegant
FRENCH

The trouble with beauty is that it's difficult to agree exactly what it is — taste and standards vary so much — but I defy anyone to disagree that Château de Christin is a most beautiful building. Originally the residence of the de Baschi family, who ruled the region in the 16th century, the château is set deep in the countryside west of the small town of Sommières in the Gard.

CROWNING GLORY

To look at, Château de Christin is really more of a large manor house than a château. Constructed from stone, in a Venetian style with the rooftop resembling a coronet, the house has a Cinderella feel about it. It was bought by the d'Urre family after the death of the last de Baschi in 1777, and it was the d'Urres who added the coronet to the roof after the French Revolution, to signal to the lower classes their connections with royal stock.

When Olivier Delafargue, a businessman, and his wife Nina arrived here from Marseille two years ago, the château was, like the glass slipper, a perfect fit. The couple live what appears to be a fairy-tale existence, although the upkeep of this building can be no mean

ABOVE *The front elevation of Château de Christin is unusual. Described as Venetian by the owners, it has a fairy-tale aura that's hard to resist.*
RIGHT *The bread oven in this huge stone fireplace in the study off the grand hallway indicates that the room was probably the original kitchen. Although no longer in use for cooking, the fireplace still throws out great heat in the winter months, burning two-metre logs of chêne blanc.*

OPPOSITE *The door to the kitchen from the dining room is cleverly disguised within the painted* boiserie *(panelling).* **ABOVE LEFT** *Detail of a 19th-century chandelier, given a quirky twist with ivory-handled cutlery by renowned French designer–decorator Richard Goullet.* **ABOVE CENTRE** *This is just a fraction of the collection of copper pans.* **ABOVE RIGHT** *Green glazed terracotta cups are commonplace in France, but this model has a delightfully unusual shape.* **BELOW RIGHT** *The white faïenceware on display does get used, but it's also for sale.*

feat. As well as being their home, it is also a hotel. There are 18 rooms in the main building, and the large stables have been converted into a separate dwelling, so a large family or bunch of friends can live their own fairy-tale for a week or two.

I have given Nina and Olivier special dispensation to appear in this book – I confess I was swayed by their beautiful home. They are not antiques dealers in the true sense, but buy and sell they do. Guests beguiled by the comfort of a *lit bateau*, the romance of dining beneath a twinkling

LEFT *Palm trees and their leaves were once symbols of victory, peace and fertility. This beautifully bound and illustrated book imparts relevant gems of wisdom.*

chandelier and the sublime experience of dozing on a 1940s iron campaign bed by the swimming pool are also given the opportunity of taking the memory home with them. Look carefully and everything – well, almost everything – has a discreet price tag.

The gardens are as spectacular as you would expect for such a grand house. Carefully tended rose beds bloom prolifically with white and pink varieties as soft as freshly spun candyfloss and with the distinctive, delicate old rose fragrance. There's also an olive grove with a large *bassin* (pond) and stone statuary, a potager with a sheltered seating area and a rose-covered walkway. Surrounded by a hedge of neatly clipped balls of box, the pool area, with its breathtaking views over the countryside, is invisible from the house.

Not many homes have their own chapel. Garlanded with cobwebs, this one appears to have few visitors. The exquisite, hand-painted wall behind the altar is truly magnificent, and would impress even the staunchest atheist. The background colour is azure-blue, reminiscent of the robe of a classical figure in a Pre-Raphaelite painting. This sumptuous shade is also picked out in the plumage of the little birds that hop nimbly from one golden tendril of ivy to the next.

LEFT *The hallway that leads to the bedrooms is wide enough for this mahogany daybed. The old school posters continue the botanical theme of the Herbalist's Suite, reached through the double doors.*

OPPOSITE *In the converted stables, the upstairs salon is vast and atmospheric. This little chair, all dressed up for the ball like Cinderella, is dwarfed by the majestic proportions of the old stone fireplace.*

THIS PAGE *The private quarters on the top floor have unusual quatrefoil mesh panels at the windows. Reproduction toile de Jouy fabric has been used to cover the 19th-century fauteuil in Nina and Olivier's bedroom.*

Since Nina and Olivier have lived at Château de Christin, they have brought their own artistic vision to bear on some of the rooms, but on such a scale and with such dedication that progress is slow. Instead of employing any random painter or decorator, they asked their close friend, the top French designer–decorator Richard Goullet, to add his distinctive touches: mixing *chaux* (limewash) to just the right shade of pink for the walls of Nina and Olivier's bedroom, so that they match exactly the colour of the old rose 'Pierre de Ronsard' growing outside, customizing chandeliers with ivory-handled knives and forks and draping a little chair with an antique linen sheet, transforming it into a couture creation worthy of Christian Dior.

The stately gothic entrance of the château leads into the hall, where visitors are greeted by an elegant birdcage, a couple of stone chickens its

ABOVE *The frescoes on this landing depict local landmarks, including the Pont du Gard. Sixty kilometres from the château, it is the most visited monument in France after the Eiffel Tower.*
LEFT *In the hallway, trophies from old hunting trips are proudly displayed. The 19th-century wire birdcage is purely decorative.*

only residents. The room to the left of the hall, functioning as an office/reception area, has a huge stone fireplace, no longer in use, but a stunning feature nevertheless. Beyond the hallway is the main salon, a formal room with satin-covered chaises longues and other comfortable seating positioned at jaunty angles under floor-to-ceiling windows, inviting one to gaze out upon the splendid gardens. To the left of this salon is a more sombre room, wood-panelled in the manner

of a gentleman's club, with deep-buttoned green leather chesterfield sofas. This is where guests retire to in the evenings, to enjoy the intoxicating contents of crystal decanters.

A grand staircase with a carpet runner – unusual for the South of France – sweeps up from the terrazzo floor in the hallway to the five guest bedrooms. Each of the rooms has a very different feel. The Herbalist's Suite is lined with botanical prints; the Blue Room, on the garden side of the building, is imbued with a different light at different times of the day. The Marquis's Room – the largest – has a splendid stuccoed ceiling, while the Bird Room at the top of the château has a glorious view over the woods, so the depicted inhabitants feel at home. There are no prizes for guessing the theme of the Tulip Room. Whichever room you choose, comfort is guaranteed.

Having bathed in one of the splendid cast-iron baths in the en-suite bathrooms, guests can then waft down to the dining room for a candlelit dinner, or in the morning take breakfast on the paved patio outside the kitchen. Just don't assume that the adorable chair you sat on the previous day will still be there – the last guests to leave may well have made a purchase.

ABOVE LEFT *The patio immediately outside the kitchen is where meals are taken during summer. It's the perfect place for flower arranging.*
ABOVE RIGHT *You need to knock loudly to arouse 14-year-old Avrile. The huge glazed terracotta pots were made in nearby Anduze.*

ABOVE *These empty glass yogurt pots have been recycled and are now used to hold tealights to illuminate the gardens at night. The unused antique birdcage is purely decorative and overgrown with Virginia creeper.*

RIGHT *This statue is one of many dotted around the gardens, although others are lucky enough to still have their heads.*

BELOW *The lean-to affords a shady seating area at the back of this secluded section of the gardens.*

ABOVE *The colour of the red-oxide glazed hexagonal tiles on the salon floor is picked out in the 19th-century paisley throw and velvet cushions on the sofa and also in the 19th-century Moroccan kilim. A beautiful melange of curiosities on the circular coffee table ranges from a faceted lump of crystal to a* **tilleul** *(limewood) pot full of burned incense sticks that leave the room filled with an exotic scent.*

OPPOSITE *The 19th-century, black lacquered bookcase contains a mini library of beautiful art books, favourite novels and family photos.*

Although he is only in his fifties, Jean-Louis Fages may be the most experienced antiques dealer you'll ever come across. Thirty years ago, he opened his first shop in the historic town of Nîmes, where he was born, and it is in Nîmes that he lives and works today.

CURIOSITY SHOP

Jean-Louis's present shop, off the Place du Crocodile in the centre of Nîmes, is crammed full of reproductions of his favourite styles and periods, primarily Louis XV and 18th century. The originals of the various pieces are becoming increasingly hard to find, probably because when Jean-Louis comes across any he keeps them!

The apartment that he shares with his partner Matthieu, a solicitor, couldn't be in a more atmospheric location. On the top floor of an 1830s building, it overlooks the Maison Carrée, a beautifully preserved Roman temple.

Matthieu is as passionate about collecting as Jean-Louis, and the pair often forage together for more curiosities with which to fill their home. Five years ago when they moved into the apartment, it was bare and bland. In a short time, they transformed it into an elegant yet comfortable home. Although there is a sense of unity among the rooms, they are all very individual, with an air of the Grand Tour about them.

A tiny black and white tiled hallway lies behind the double-door entrance to the apartment. All the rooms, which lead off one another, have floor-

to-ceiling French windows opening onto a balcony that runs around the entire apartment. Large planted pots create a city garden that looks down onto tiny, quiet streets on one side and the main boulevard of Nîmes on the other.

The main salon, like all the other rooms, has been decorated with absolute confidence, its whimsical touches offset by masculine detailing. The large, curvaceous sofa, for example, is boldly upholstered in a biscuit-coloured checked linen, while a leopard skin has been draped over the back. Matthieu often works from home, studying legal manuscripts, so every room has a place to sit, read and take notes. In this room, work space is provided by the long beech dining table, set in front of the large, black lacquered bookcase.

In some ways, this room is like a museum; everything is precious and fascinating, but not so precious that it can't be handled or admired. The original floor-to-ceiling built-in cupboards,

BELOW *The red velvet upholstered* lit de repos *in the study is Louis XVI. Classical in style, it becomes welcoming when stacked with cushions. The classical theme continues in the exquisite large engraving in a heavy gilt frame above.*

OPPOSITE *A collection of crystal decanters with tiny lead dogs, including pugs — the owners' favourite breed (above). A detail of the iron bird on the standard lamp (below). The blue paint highlights the 1850s English mahogany tallboy (right).*

THIS PAGE *In an Indian birdcage in the dining room lives a tiny goldfinch, whose song mimics the door bell (left). A fraction of the owners' 18th- and 19th- century and contemporary creamware and silverware (top right). A treasured childhood gift, this adorable little donkey has a mechanical tail that makes his ears move! (below right). Walnuts and fruit on a rustic table make casual reference to an old master still life (bottom right).*

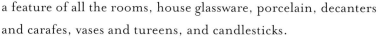

a feature of all the rooms, house glassware, porcelain, decanters and carafes, vases and tureens, and candlesticks.

Lighting is one of Jean-Louis's specialities, with bespoke lampshades making up a significant part of his business. As you might expect, the lighting throughout the apartment is carefully considered: lamps are angled to precision and controlled by remote, chandeliers are on dimmers, while candlelight plays an important part in creating just the right atmosphere.

The next room, the study, is painted a vibrant blue called Sainte Vierge. Despite the colour, the room has the restrained feel of an English gentleman's club. There are some fine 18th-century English mahogany pieces here – the couple are almost as passionate about this period as they are about Louis XV. A red velvet Louis XVI *lit de repos* is a favourite snoozing place of the

OPPOSITE *Diners are watched over by the stern, earringed corsair in the fine 18th-century French oil painting in a simple gilt frame. The 19th-century French ormolu and crystal chandelier lends a light magical touch.*

couple's two adored pugs. These privileged canines are a frequent but subtle motif repeated through the apartment, represented in silk on cushions, drawings on paper or as tiny lead models.

The apple-green dining room is home to a tiny goldfinch with a beautiful song that manages to confuse everyone with its quirky mimicry of the doorbell. The furniture is a melange of styles and epochs – an English pedestal mahogany dining table, a modern console table, a French bronze and crystal chandelier – all living together harmoniously, while retaining a very French feel.

Although small, the kitchen is the hub of the home. This compact room is full of beautiful 19th-century apothecary jars, marble mortars and pestles, and white ceramic confit jars. All these beautiful objects are not just for display; they are in everyday use. Similarly, aromatic thyme, parsley, sage and rosemary plants massed in terracotta pots on the little terrace just off the kitchen are used every day for cooking.

No sooner do you set foot inside than you realize that there is no pastiche or plagiarism *chez* Fages. An undeniable and enviable balance of accessibility and elegance, this comfortable, lived-in home is an original, functioning cabinet of curiosities where nothing is out of bounds.

ABOVE LEFT *The small kitchen has enough space for a table for lunches* à deux. **LEFT** *Know your onions and display them well!* **OPPOSITE ABOVE LEFT** *With magnets fitted to their bases, these pots of spices double as an installation.* **OPPOSITE ABOVE RIGHT** *Above the kitchen table is a 17th-century Dutch chandelier, a family heirloom.* **OPPOSITE BELOW LEFT** *A stack of antique linen sheets with lace edging.* **OPPOSITE BELOW RIGHT** *In the utility room, curtains on a rod are an alternative to cupboard doors.*

Franck Delmarcelle lives an enviable life. For him, his work is his passion, so living to work, rather than the other way round, is exactly the way he likes it. Home and work blend into one, with his elegant Paris apartment and antiques shop just five minutes' walk apart.

CURIOUS CREATURES

Franck Delmarcelle's antiques shop, Galerie Et Caetera, which opened in 1998, is on rue de Poitou in the Marais. The shop's opening hours are restricted, or you can visit by appointment. This isn't an affectation, for Franck has his fingers in many other pies, perhaps entertaining a customer at his home or doing what all dealers do best – getting out there and sourcing more pieces for his shop and home.

Franck is to antiques what Christian Lacroix is to fashion – there are no concepts, just an emotional response to the visual world; a mixing and matching of styles and objects. He is also a skilled interior decorator, always in demand and forever being asked by hip glossies to supply props for fashion shoots.

Franck's partner in life is Laurent Dombrowicz, a well-known and well-respected figure in the world of fashion. Like many in the city, they rent their apartment.

RIGHT *Chunky balustrading has been converted into a pair of table lamps, positioned at either end of the salon table. The eclectic display includes a glass dome holding dried hydrangeas, two fossilized stones resembling faces, a petrified horse's head, a stuffed cat and a religious figure. Behind, four architectural prints lean against the wall.*

One of ten in a building that's part 18th century, part 19th, at about 120 square metres it's large by Parisian standards. Even though they don't own their home and have lived there for a relatively short time, the couple have transformed the interior with their distinctive style.

The hall is the first of seven rooms, each one leading off the next, all of them spacious. The black and white tiled floor continues into the kitchen and is repeated in the bathroom. The hall is large enough to hold substantial pieces of furniture, including a classic 18th-century embroidered sofa, which still has a price tag attached (has it just arrived from the shop or is it on its way out to a buyer?). It's almost hidden

OPPOSITE *During the winter, fires in the white marble fireplace in the salon are puffed to a roar with a pair of bellows adorned with a real tortoise shell. Another tortoise sits in front of three 18th-century mirrors on the mantelpiece.* **ABOVE** *His and his red velvet cushions are a bold splash of colour in the bedroom.* **BELOW** *Perfect symmetry gives the salon a Libran balance.*

ABOVE LEFT *A large, 17th-century Flemish carved wood reliquary of a caped St Anthony in the dining room.* **CENTRE** *Detail of figs on the dining table.* **ABOVE RIGHT** *The glazed cabinet in the dining room is crammed full of stuffed birds, still with their beautiful plumage.* **OPPOSITE** *An 18th-century Swedish rustic table and four chairs with crumpled, drop-in leather seats stand on herringbone parquet flooring. They all have a rich patina in common, in contrast to the sleek new paint on the floor-to-ceiling, bespoke display case.*

from view though, piled high with motorcycle helmets, catwalk outfits, lots of black coats and even more black boots on the floor.

The couple's aesthetic is catholic in every sense. Both bizarre and beautiful, the decorative objects in the apartment range from a Patagonian taxidermied hare, collections of mercury glass, concrete toadstools, a desk lamp made from a girl's ribcage, stuffed birds on perches and a gilded tole sacred heart. Stuffed creatures and religious iconography feature throughout. For Franck and Laurent, taxidermy is not in any way macabre, rather it allows the beauty of birds and animals to

be appreciated after death. Similarly, their love of iconograpy is not to do with personal religious beliefs but their appreciation of the art and emotion of the craftsmen who made the pieces.

There is an eclectic mix of styles of furniture in the first main room, a study-cum-guest room, including a rustic table, an ornate painted baroque desk, two Louis XV chairs and a *lit de repos* with a metal frame over the top made by Franck. In the more pared-down dining room, a custom-built glazed unit spans the length and height of one wall. Made from reclaimed materials with accents of gold leaf and lit with strands of fairy lights, it

houses even more unusual collections that merge into a harmonious but disparate whole – from pieces of coral, shells, butterflies and a giant cockroach carapace to a child's model Citroën from the 1950s that conceals an iPod dock on permanent shuffle and more iconography and stuffed animals. Books, magazines and CDs are stored in the cupboards at the bottom. The blue painted walls create an aura of calm refinement and are the perfect backdrop for the 18th-century Swedish dining table and chairs. A severe but exquisite late 17th-century Flemish wooden reliquary of St Anthony atop a very simple 19th-century table presides over the room.

There is a distinctly Belgian look to the next room – the salon; no great surprise when you discover that Laurent was born in Belgium. The walls are painted a confident shade of brown-grey, and beautiful terracotta hexagonal tiles cover the floor. The roughly hewn shutters are made from reclaimed scaffolding boards, a brave contrast to the chic upholstered sofas, while the use of garden statuary indoors makes a confident statement. The collections of *objets morts* continue in this room, the highlights being a stuffed porcupine with vicious spines and a rare Pacific turtle.

Clever use has been made of space in the compact bedroom. The panelling behind the bed appears purely decorative but, in fact, it conceals cupboards in which all the paraphernalia of the *chambre* is hidden. Apart from the bed, the only other piece of furniture is a cane seat spanning the

width of the window wall, which is fittted with more salvaged shutters. The room is uncluttered and unadorned, perfect for sleeping.

Although most of us would not want to leave this magical apartment, whenever they can Franck and Laurent visit their *maison de vacances* in Lesay, Picardy. Close by is the *chambre d'hôte* they are renovating, which promises to be as successful as all the other properties they have touched with their unique vision. Their collection of *objets morts* is sure to grow and fill the shelves here. Guests should expect the unexpected…

OPPOSITE *The blue of the dining room is the perfect backdrop to the gilt-and-black framed pictures and mirrors displayed tightly around the fireplace. The Wedgwood plaque depicting Justice is an identical blue, as are the subtle highlights on the tall candlesticks. Make no mistake — this is not coincidence but experienced styling.* **ABOVE** *Detail of coral in a cast-iron French garden urn.*

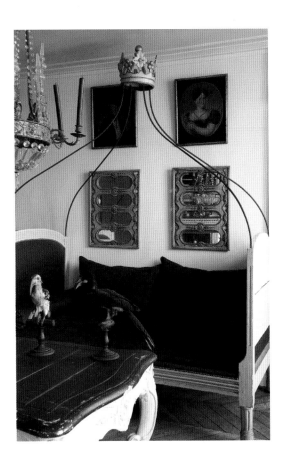

ABOVE *The 19th-century daybed in the study has been cleverly customized by Franck, with an iron frame topped by a carved and gilded crown.* **RIGHT** *Carved statuary pitted by rains, blistered by summer sun and then crackled by Jack Frost slowly gains a patina over the decades that's impossible to recreate. This classical figure with an urn must be glad to have been brought in from the elements.* **OPPOSITE** *Franck and Laurent's obsession with* **objets morts** *is not in the least macabre.* **Au contraire.** *Instead, they find true beauty in the impressive collection of stuffed birds and taxidermied beasts that are present throughout the apartment. Like the characters in the cult film* **Harold and Maude,** *they have a great regard for the dead. Their motto is 'Love awards beauty'.*

In my opinion, Spencer Swaffer is the most successful antiques dealer in the UK today. Before I joined the trade, my Suffolk friends, who had been a part of it for all their lives, used to regale me with their antiquing tales. They always spoke admiringly of Spencer, of his amazing eye and boundless energy.

FLOWER POWER

With any fair that you might visit across the UK and in France, too, you can bet that Spencer has got there first, slapping his trademark 'SOLD' label onto the best of everything. The label depicts the front of his exquisite, bow-fronted Elizabethan shop in the centre of Arundel, West Sussex, which is where all his purchases end up before being sold to an international roster of discerning dealers, decorators and homeowners.

LEFT *The main living room is a harmonious mix of the couple's tastes. The lampshades came from nearby Charleston Farmhouse. The Bagues rock crystal wall lights, while extremely valuable, do not look out of place in this cosy room.* **BELOW** *Prevent Spencer Swaffer from going to an antiques fair, and he would be a fish out of water.*

THIS PAGE *This 1920s Italian sconce is one of the first purchases Spencer made when he started going on buying trips to France.*
OPPOSITE ABOVE *The delicate chandelier is an example of the sort of lighting that Spencer stocks in his shop. The dining chairs are English, from the reign of William IV.*
OPPOSITE BELOW *'God has sown his name on the heavens in glittering stars, but on earth He planteth His name by tender flowers.'*
Jean Paul Richter (1763–1825)

Born in Brighton, Spencer has dealt in antiques since the age of 12. He was a lonely child, kicking pebbles on beaches and hiking across the South Downs, collecting stones and shells on his way. Jumble sales were a dream come true for him, and he set up a museum in his bedroom to showcase his purchases. In 1962, the Home Service got wind of this peculiar little boy, and Jack de Manio interviewed him on the equivalent of the *Today* programme. A savvy antiques dealer heard the story and hightailed it to his bedroom door, where Spencer was charging 2d for entry to his museum. The dealer offered him £50 for a couple of his treasures, and the rest is history. Spencer's parents died when he was 20; he sold their cottage and bought his present shop. That was in 1974, and he is dealing in Arundel to this day.

ABOVE LEFT *These old French gilt metal letters induce peaceful slumber in the guest bedroom.* CENTRE *A collection of* paniers de fleurs *from the bases of console tables has been artfully arranged on the bathroom wall.* ABOVE RIGHT *Architectural cornicing, strong enough to take the weight of jars filled with shells and stones, has become a shelf running around the bathroom.* OPPOSITE *Even the study in this house is not free of flower paintings. The sycamore chair, from around 1900, was once used by loom workers at a Lancashire cotton mill.*

The shop is a most beautiful building, built in 1580 and originally an inn. Four floors are full of tasteful stock, and the turnover is fast. The same loyal staff have been with him for years; the sign of a good boss. They are on first-name terms with all their clients, who are always welcomed with coffee, tea or a glass of wine, depending on the time of day. The garden out back is no less than breathtaking. Mature and well cared for, it contains a Romanesque font enjoying a second life as a fountain and garden statuary, creating the feel of a grand country house. The protective high brick walls – actually the walls of Arundel Castle – encourage a microclimate that allows subtropical plants to thrive.

Spencer's home, which he shares with his pretty, vivacious wife Freya, is grand, too, and also in Arundel, meaning that it's just a short walk to work. The majority of houses in the town are of

red brick and 18th- and 19th-century construction, and Spencer's detached double-fronted George I townhouse is no exception. With its shiny red door, white columns and palm trees, one might expect to find a formal interior, but, as with all antiques dealers, their homes tend to reflect their shops and stock, and Spencer's conforms to this stereotype.

In all homes, from time to time, objects get replaced for purely asethetic reasons, but in the homes of antiques dealers, this upgrading occurs with alarming regularity. Whenever a better model comes along, the old version is swiftly traded up and sent back to the shop. But there comes a time when change becomes less exhilarating, and in Spencer's case, his home has reached perfection. Though sparser and more ethnic in feel than his shop, and with a distinct Bloomsbury touch, this is, without doubt, the home of the top dealer.

ABOVE LEFT *These distinctive animal jugs are fine examples of the type of glazed terracotta pottery produced in the Toulouse area in the early 19th century.* ABOVE RIGHT *The Bloomsbury theme is alive and well in this collection of unframed canvases in the kitchen.* BELOW *A real-life still life, with a painting of a terracotta watering jug in the background.* OPPOSITE ABOVE *19th-century wine bin labels from a Burgundy wine cellar.* OPPOSITE BELOW *The house has underground cellars, one of which is lined with a fitted wine rack.*

Double-fronted houses have a perfect symmetry – ask a child to draw a house and he or she will place the door in the middle, with windows either side. These houses are the most comfortable to live in, with plenty of ground-floor space and a choice of turning either left or right on entering, giving a sense of balance. Off the hall to the right is the dining room, which has a simple, elegant bookcase, with soft gothic arches in the glazing. To the left is the comfortable Bloomsburyesque living room.

The kitchen is a continuation of the living room. If you feel grumpy, look up and read the large gilt letters stuck above the entrance: 'S.M.I.L.E.'. How could you not? This house has a wonderful serenity – it's no surprise to learn that Freya practises yoga every day in the beautifully sparse bedroom in front of floor-to-ceiling windows fitted with elegant, colonial-style shutters.

Freya adores flowers. In the kitchen, there is a large collection of still lifes of posies and arrangements, many unframed. Maybe among these treasures is an undiscovered Vanessa Bell? The lovingly tended garden at the back of the house is the source of the monkshood and sweet peas artfully arranged in confit jars and pots in the kitchen. The garden is not just ornamental – the potager produces all the vegetables the Swaffers eat.

A few years ago, Spencer lost the sight in one eye, but he is never offended if anyone jokes that he's always had a good eye. Perhaps it's something to do with all the carrots he eats!

THIS PAGE *The raspberry ripple-coloured ornate iron gate (top left) leads from the garden to the brick-built conservatory, where succulents grow abundantly in old marble mortars (top right), heirloom tomatoes ripen (below left) and an abundant crop of red onions is left out to dry (bottom left). This oil painting (below) is an artistic impression of a Sanderson paint chart, with daubs of harmonizing colour applied by thumbprint.*
OPPOSITE *The main focus of the pretty conservatory is this grand pair of ornate antique French doors, given a whole new lease of life with the clever use of mirrors slotted behind the decorative iron panelling depicting thistles.*

*Everything about Christine Nossereau exudes beauty
— not only is she is stunning to look at but she also
has impeccable taste. This becomes all too clear when
you visit her exclusive shop and home, both in the
picturesque Provençal town of L'Isle sur la Sorgue.
Antiques are big business in this extraordinary little
town. Outside of Paris, there are more dealers here
than in the rest of France put together.*

ANIMAL MAGIC

The River Sorgue, with ancient watermills lining its
banks, winds through the town. Along one bank, there
are bars, cafés and restaurants, which are always busy,
while on the opposite bank is one antiques shop after
another, selling everything from 17th-century church
relics to 1960s Vallauris pottery. Every Sunday, there
is a bustling market in the centre of Sorgue, where
a seductive range of antiques is for sale, alongside
mouthwatering Provençal delicacies, clothes and crafts.
Every Easter and towards the middle of August, a market
devoted to antiques fills the famous Parc Gautier and
spills out onto all the streets. The atmosphere is
fabulous, if you're into antiques, that is.

ABOVE *Laden with quirky decorative pieces. the marble-topped,
cabriole-legged table just inside the front door has little space for keys.
An urn with a faux tole cactus teasingly pricks a mannequin's hand.*
LEFT *The only seating in the crammed menagerie of a kitchen is two
bar stools, just enough for enjoying a quick café express.* **OPPOSITE** *The
family room is equipped for repose with a modern sofa, a deep-buttoned
leather chesterfield and an 18th-century French fauteuil.*

LEFT *An 18th-century Swedish drop-leaf table in the hallway, with original blue paint, is crammed to distraction, in a John Soane kind of way, with an array of classical figures in plaster or carved wood. Their soft putty shades are the same as the crumpled, vellum-bound books.* **ABOVE** *Antiques dealers drive either Volvo estates or Mercedes vans — you just can't get a chest of drawers in a Citroën Deux Chevaux! It's just as well Christine drives a Merc for this troop of horses.*

Christine's unerring eye means that her shop contains the very best examples of everything, from fine floor-to-ceiling carved Corinthian columns and exquisite 17th-century Italian mirrors to 18th-century marriage armoires and lots and lots of wooden horses.

As you'd expect, Christine's home, which she shares with her architect husband Denis and, from time to time, their son Thibault, is also full of these perfect examples. (Thibault, who has inherited his parents' *goût impeccable*, is also an antiques dealer, with a space at the famous Marché Paul Bert in Paris.) Unusual for Sorgue, their large family house, built at the end of the 19th century, has a large garden to match.

The Nossereaus are trendsetters, and Christine's own unique way of combining and displaying objects to create just the right effect has inspired many to follow in her footsteps. If imitation is truly the sincerest form of flattery, Christine should feel very flattered, but it must be said that no one does what she does quite so well.

In spite of her good looks, Christine is not keen on having her photograph taken, but she was incredibly open and welcoming when it came to showing her vast collection of treasures to our camera. Animals loom large throughout the

ABOVE LEFT *A collection of miniature donkeys. If you look at the back of any donkey, you will see that he carries the sign of the cross.*
LEFT *The upstairs landing is illuminated by a chandelier made from fairy lights.*

OPPOSITE *Visiting guests have to be prepared to share when they stay the night — the recumbent female is a permanent resident on this old shepherd's bed, with its antique linen-covered, deep-buttoned mattress.*

house, nowhere more so than in the kitchen, which is home to images of cats on metal advertising signs, paintings of horses ploughing the land and tin models of cows. However, it's still a functioning kitchen, complete with a black Lacanche oven against a wall of original, crackle-glazed white tiles.

Christine loves horses and is an accomplished rider, so it comes as no real surprise to find that there is an equine theme running through the house. In the hall, on top of the 18th-century Chinese cupboard, still with its original patina, there are no less than nine carved and painted horses, and there are plenty more on the floor. Mounted on the wall is a huge plaster cast of a horse's head – majestic and imposing.

The largest room in the house is the dining room. Shuttered windows at each end allow in dappled light through the thick,

overgrown ampelopsis that covers the exterior. The long,
18th-century Italian dining table is laden with silver trays,
a papier-mâché camel (a recent wedding anniversary gift from
Denis to Christine), carved candesticks and crystal decanters.
Dining here in winter, seated on the 18th-century Swedish
chairs, is a spectacle reminiscent of scenes from *Babette's Feast*.

OPPOSITE ABOVE *In the main bedroom, it is all threes: three austere mannequin
heads sit in front of three crumbly, ornate carved Italian candlesticks on a bedside
table.* **OPPOSITE BELOW** *The modern triptych painting hanging above the bed
functions as a visual headboard.* **ABOVE** *See no evil, hear no evil, speak no evil!*
RIGHT *East-facing, the main bathroom is drowned in early morning sunlight.
The soft furnishings — bags, floor mats and chair coverings — were all made from
antique linen by the local creative duo Les Habits 9.*

Also on the ground floor is a comfortable and cosy family room, with a large, deep, buttoned leather sofa and a chandelier mobile of notes, postcards and invitations by Ingo Maurer. This room leads to *la pièce d'inspiration*: a workshop/office, where fragments of wood and scraps of fabric are used to give new life to damaged pieces, and parts of dolls await tender loving care and restoration before they are moved to the shop.

On the floor above, reached by two separate red-oxide tiled staircases, there are seven more rooms and even more animals scattered throughout, including horses, camels and the most adorable collection of miniature donkeys. The guest bedroom contains a bed that once belonged to a shepherd who used it for his siestas, and a carved polychrome sculpture of a sleeping woman is a permanent resident. Except for the triptych of paintings above the master bed, painted by the couple's friend and local artist Zénitran, the bathrooms and lighting offer the only modern touches on this floor.

A large pergola-covered decked terrace runs the entire width of the back of the house. Whenever the weather allows, meals are taken here on the zinc-topped table, often in the company of a large, crown-wearing stuffed toad that sits on the table like a bewitched king on a lily pad. The garden is lush and green, even in the heat of the scorching

LEFT *The large workshop/office at the back of the house looks out onto the garden and is always bathed in natural light. The huge refectory table is a dolls' hospital of arms and heads, together with other flotsam and jetsam, pebbles and stones, either waiting restoration or creative transformation. The blue boat Providence on the enormous draper's dresser base is from a fairground.*

LEFT AND BELOW LEFT *Two cool, shaded pockets of calm in the garden offer a choice for summer relaxation. Under a wisteria-clad pergola, the round table with four chairs is perfect for informal shared lunches. The rabbit's quarters (below) is more conducive to solitary reflection.* **ABOVE** *Detail of the zinc-topped table on the terrace, with a crowned stuffed toad bringing a fairy-tale edge to the scene.* **OPPOSITE** *The decked dining terrace is a room in itself. A pergola covered with mature climbers helps keep it cool in the height of summer.*

summers that are normal in this corner of France. A raised swimming pool and a couple of shaded corners allow for cooling off and quiet reflection, but there are also areas for basking in the sun. The animal theme continues outdoors: an alert white stone rabbit surveys the garden from an old metal bistro table, while a carved wooden ram in a huge iron frame, a rare 19th-century piece of *art forain* (fairground art), stands alone beneath a weeping willow.

Since photographing their home and writing this piece, the Nossereaus have moved to Normandy. The north of France will now benefit from what they have to offer, but no doubt their loyal customers will follow and the antique menagerie will enjoy the new pastures. All is not lost, though, for those visting L'Isle sur la Sorgue – the new owners of the house are offering a *chambre d'hôte* so that others can stay and enjoy this calm oasis.

Eclectic FRENCH

La Fabrique is set deep in the French countryside in a lush, green valley, with a fast-flowing river running alongside. From the outside, the building looms up, large and imposing, giving no indication of the chic and whimsical family home inside.

RUN OF THE MILL

La Fabrique is enormous. The home (and antiques business) of Bernard and Maxime Cassagnes was originally a paper mill, hence its size. Bernard, a trained architect, bought the 1890s mill in its original state and moved there in 1981; Max, his bohemian wife, joined him in 1985. Using his architectural skills and unerring eye, Bernard has created a truly remarkable and unusual home.

Famous in the trade as Le Baron, a term of affection given to him by his fellow architecture students, Bernard runs his antiques business from the mill. His speciality is *art forain* – fairground art – and there are plenty of examples in the shop, as well as in the living space, but he deals in all things large, strange and beautiful.

The couple live in only a small section of the building, although the ghosts of the mill workers seem ever-present in the *cave* beneath the living accommodation. This huge vaulted cellar is where Bernard stores his restoration equipment, from piles of wood and crates of chair springs to sheets of mirror and antique glass panels. Small in stature but larger than life, Bernard is passionate

OPPOSITE ABOVE *The life-size horse and rider in the corner of the main salon give an indication of the enormous scale of this room. The gallant-looking chap is swigging Vin tonique de la Durante out of his boot.* **OPPOSITE BELOW** *A 19th-century French mahogany display case, with an array of stuffed exotic birds.* **ABOVE** *Trained architect Bernard painted this room himself. This is where the family gathers after dinner, perhaps to watch the television, which is discreetly concealed behind the large panel doors.*

ABOVE LEFT *The top of a chocolatier's display piece. The metal figures dance for joy, as do the scantily clad ladies beneath.* **ABOVE CENTRE** *The staircase makes a dramatic turn in front of a window festooned with cobwebs.* **ABOVE RIGHT** *The imposing plaster statue of Mark Antony was originally a theatre prop.*

about his collections and never throws anything away, believing that there's a use for everything.

The faded red front door with a Georgian fanlight opens onto a gargantuan hallway, where you are greeted by a giant-sized plaster theatre prop of the Roman general Mark Antony. The ground floor is shop space, complete with a *pou du ciel* (flying flea) aeroplane and a church organ.

A sweeping staircase with beautiful, aged wooden treads leads to a small door to the living space, with a discreet notice requesting incomers to *Essuyez vos pieds* (Wipe your feet). Although taking up only a fraction of the mill, the living space is vast. Absolutely immaculate, it is in contrast to those areas used as work, storage or shop space, and equally, if not more, beguiling.

In the kitchen/breakfast room/dining room, collections of stuffed reptiles cling to the back of the door, while the mix of wine and beautiful glass apothecary bottles displayed on a shelf beneath a stuffed fish is the lightest decorative touch. The main dining table is covered with a 19th-century yellow embroidered cloth from Morocco. The disguise is appropriate for more sensitive diners – the table was originally an operating table – but for those with a hospital background, it is only partial, because the pedals are still visible. To complete the scene, there is an operating theatre light above. Outside the window is a long cord attached to a brass bell that Max pulls to summon Bernard to the phone or for dinner. Off this room, an enormous terrace overlooks the river where Max swims in the summer.

The grand salon is, as its name might suggest, the biggest room of all, with a beautiful polished wood floor, which means that shoes are forbidden. It is dominated by a coffee table made from a roulette board of inlaid wood, covered with glass for protection. Even the humdrum is disguised to look attractive: the television is hidden behind tall double doors, and the heater on the window wall is covered by an ornate ironwork grille. This originally formed part of the Art Nouveau arch above the entrance to one of the Paris Metro stations, designed by Hector Guimard in 1900. All this is presided over by a 1930s life-size equestrian statue of Maréchal de Bassompierre, used as an advertising emblem for Vin tonique de la Durante.

Climbing the creaky staircase to the next floor, one is greeted by two stuffed lions flanking a door. With their back halves missing, they look as if they're emerging through the wall. As you go

OPPOSITE BELOW *In between the functioning end of the kitchen and the main dining room is this cosier breakfasting area. Bowls of coffee and chunks of bread are consumed at the marble table for two before another busy day at the mill.*

ABOVE *The white-tiled kitchen has a clinical feel: utilitarian, practical and low-maintenance. A butcher's rack of hooks is used to hang colanders and saucepans, while all is illuminated by an operating theatre lamp.*

ABOVE LEFT *This original cast-iron tub brings to mind the famous painting by David that depicts Marat, the French revolutionary leader, murdered in his bath.* **ABOVE RIGHT** *In the simple, elegant upstairs bathroom, a deep claw-footed antique tub invites one to take a long and luxurious soak while enjoying the view of the garden and the river beneath.* **BELOW** *Long before the arrival of the euro, cafés across France used to return change on these little saucers indicating the correct amount. This one has been reincarnated as a soap dish.*

through the door, you feel as though you're entering the world of Narnia. Eight rooms, including bedrooms, Max's studio and a huge bathroom, lead off the long corridor.

The magnificent slate-floored bathroom has a bank of four basins set in marble and lit by bare-bulb lights, creating the magical feel of a theatre dressing room. The claw-foot, cast-iron bath offers an unobstructed view of the river and countryside beyond – utterly romantic. If time is short, there's also a walk-in shower with antique fittings and slate walls. The equally impressive bathroom on the ground floor has ochre-yellow walls and an enormous red, antique cast-iron slipper bath.

THIS PAGE *It's showtime in this extraordinary bathroom when the little globe lights are illuminated. A shop counter has been fitted with no less than four shiny basins, above which there are three beautifully hand-bevelled 19th-century mirrors.*

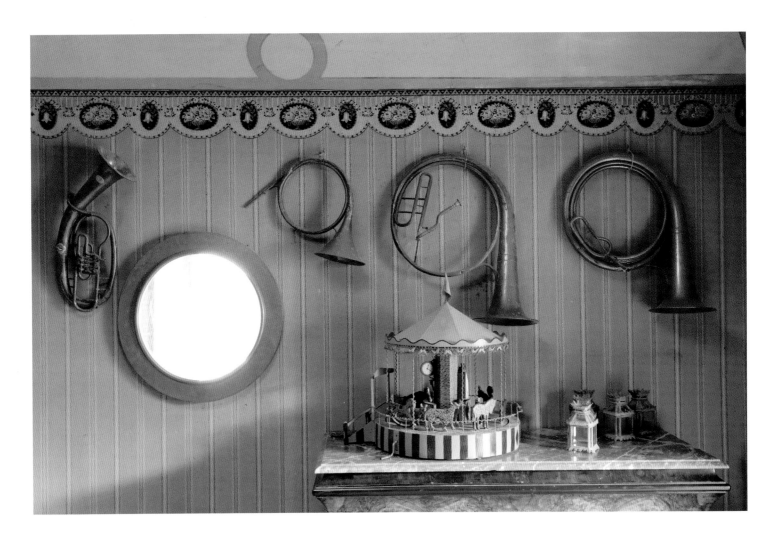

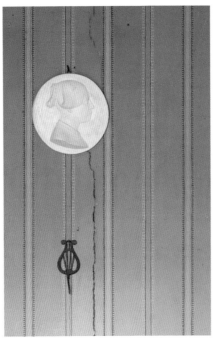

ABOVE *In the guest room, a collection of musical instruments, dulled from years of neglect, are hung on the wall like paintings.* **FAR LEFT** *The unicorn on the 19th-century toy carousel seen above. This charming model is rare and valuable.* **LEFT** *The fine hand-printed wallpaper is now elegantly faded and slightly shabby.* **OPPOSITE ABOVE** *The main bedroom is calm and intimate. With low ceilings and panelling, there is little to distract from slumber except a large painting, dating from 1900, depicting a hunting scene.* **OPPOSITE BELOW** *The strange-looking contraption on the 19th-century occasional table is a broken marine globe c. 1900.*

The master bedroom has an intimate feel, with beautiful wide wood floorboards and subtle paintwork in cream and yellow. The conservatory off the room, a 1920s addition, is home to Max's impressive collection of orchids and pelargoniums. The windowless guest room is illuminated by a huge, square skylight. An eccentric collection of antique musical instruments is displayed on one of the walls, beneath which there is a beautiful miniature carousel.

Max's studio is reached through two impressive Art Nouveau doors and by tripping across a seemingly enchanted doormat. One step on it and the lights go on; step on it again as you leave and the lights go out!

Antiques dealers could be described as the last gypsies or consummate recyclers, and Bernard must be the ultimate example of both. Although a self-confessed hoarder, he has a sophisticated eye, which is immediately apparent as you step through from the business part of the mill to their elegant home.

LEFT *In this moody unframed black and white photograph from the 1960s, Maxime cuts an enigmatic figure, rather like a character in a Godard film.* **ABOVE** *Jars of jewel-like, soft and powdery pigment are lined up upon the shelves of this bookcase.* **BELOW** *These highly stylized paintings (originally from a café in the famous Place du Capitole in Toulouse) are not the work of Maxime but an artist from the 1930s.*

THIS PAGE *Pelargoniums, orchids and rubber plants thrive in this conservatory on the second floor of the main building.*

Despite its name, La Petite Maison on the rue Paul Bert (the centre of the Paris antiques trade) is not at all small. Its proprietor, Stéphane Olivier, is a dynamic man for all seasons, and his antiques dealing has developed organically into a parallel career as a sought-after interior decorator.

A LITTLE HOUSE IN PARIS

La Petite Maison is quite unique in that it is both Stéphane's shop, showcasing his carefully chosen and arranged finds, as well as his home. With an impressive client list, Stéphane is frequently asked not just to source the perfect piece for his clients but also to tell them exactly where to put it!

Born in the foothills of the Alps, Stéphane grew up with a love and appreciation of nature, and his greatest pleasure even now is to find objects that speak with great emotion to him. So it is that, in his home, the glamorous and expensive sit cheek by jowl with the simple things in life; objects that have no value except their intrinsic beauty. He likes to mix eras, styles and materials, gathering collections of butterflies, starched shirt collars, cards of mother-of-pearl buttons and fragile coral, and displaying them under glass domes to maximum effect. As it was for the great Victorian collectors, the display of such collections is as important as the content, and Stéphane's individual take on this art has become his signature item of stock.

Just next door to the legendary Bistrot Paul Bert, the house is ivy clad and somehow reminiscent of Hansel and Gretel's

OPPOSITE *This tableau is the ultimate example of how to use symmetry to combine objects of completely different styles and from different eras. Framed dried flowers hang in a grid above a Swedish buffet flanked by a pair of 1970s Perspex standard lamps. In front sits a pair of French giltwood fauteuils awaiting reupholstery.* **ABOVE RIGHT** *In the bedroom, French marble-topped butcher's tables now play host to mercury glass finials and a scattering of curious metal polyhedrons.* **TOP** *Detail of a branch of coral with a now-defunct fob watch.*

ABOVE *In the salon/showroom, a perky white stone bird stands among a collection of green glazed terracotta vessels. Time has stopped on the huge metal clockface on the wall behind.* **LEFT** *Delicately painted edelweiss adorns the back of this 19th-century Eastern European chair.* **OPPOSITE** *Mirror, mirror on the wall, who's the fairest of them all? These large, white-painted zinc frames awaiting mirrors have a fairy-tale magic. The stalagmite configurations on the zinc-topped florists' bench were once used for flower displays.*

cottage. Four granite steps lead up to a little red door, and the atmosphere is so peaceful that it's hard to believe that this isn't a purely private domain. However, when the swinging grey shop sign is hung out on a Saturday and Sunday, it's an indication that Stéphane is open for business. His clientèle are a varied bunch, always discerning and appreciative of Stéphane's meticulous styling. They're rarely able to resist temptation, and even if they don't buy anything there and then, they never leave without making at least a pledge to purchase.

LEFT *In the rear of the salon/showroom, overlooking the dappled garden, a mix of styles of furniture is confidently displayed. They're all beautiful, high-quality pieces, ranging from an unusual metal bench and table and a large, ornate, gilt chandelier to a painted chest of drawers and an all-glass Venetian mirror.* **BELOW LEFT** *A pair of cold-painted bronze figures of two of man's best friends.*

Stéphane first opened La Petite Maison in 2000. Its success has led to a further outlet on the Left Bank on rue de l'Université, among the most chic of Paris's upmarket shops. This 'Little House' really is a home, but one where all the furniture is for sale and has a very discreet price tag attached. The turnover is huge, so it's all change every week. Stéphane and his team are consummate professionals, and the business runs like clockwork. During the weekdays, the shop is shut and that's when the endless experimentation, deliberations and rearrangements take place.

The ground floor of the house consists of one large room – the salon/showroom – which is divided into four distinct areas. Various pieces for sale, both large and small, are on display here, but the room doesn't feel at all crowded, in spite of the not-very-high ceilings. The finish on the walls is a specialized effect vaguely resembling verdigris – a rich greeny grey shade, with a hint of ochre.

Through the back windows of the salon, the large, mysterious garden beckons, invitingly dappled and shaded. Reached by a little wooden staircase, you're in for a big surprise, for every urn that ever there was you're sure to find it here. The garden is shaded by clumps of tall and willowy bamboos that move gently in the slightest breeze.

The whole effect is of a secluded woodland dell, complete with staddle stones, Arras garden benches, stone animals – you won't find a bear, but maybe a deer – and, of course, the urns.

Down another level is the cosy basement kitchen and den, which blend into one. An interior wall is completely lined with faded grey shutters – an innovative way to create the effect of panelling – and is decorated with an array of paintings, still lifes and mirrors. A bookcase is packed with design, architecture and interiors books. Stéphane's eye for the quirky and unusual is all too apparent here as well – on a low coffee table there is a particularly interesting display of treen (small objects carved in wood), best appreciated while lounging in two brown leather club armchairs.

ABOVE LEFT *The 'S' above the bed may stand for sleep, successful or Stéphane — and all would be correct! The mad eclectic assortment in the blue bedroom is a shining star of styling.*
ABOVE RIGHT *A beautiful study in oil of a naked boy playing the flute almost fills the bathroom wall.*

In the window at the front of the salon on a metal chest are three of the display domes that Stéphane is famous for. The iridescent blue in the butterflies' wings and the gleam on the glass make it look as though the insects are ready to take flight. Alongside, three silver mercury glass balls mounted on vintage wooden stands bask in the sunshine.

ABOVE LEFT *Spoilt for choice — there are no less than nine urns in different shapes, sizes and materials.* ABOVE CENTRE *A battered 19th-century French copper watering can.* ABOVE RIGHT *The welcoming façade of La Petite Maison.* BELOW *A collection of six moss-covered staddle stones, likely to be 18th century. Staddle stones were originally made to support agricultural buildings, such as granaries, a few feet off the ground, to prevent rot or infestation. Their toadstool-like appearance makes them perfect garden ornamentation.*

The top floor of the house is private space. Stéphane's bedroom feels like a cosy winter chalet. A painted dresser has a huge collection of mercury glass objects in the form of candlesticks and Madonnas. An enamel letter 'S', hanging above the bed, serves to remind Stéphane that this is where he sleeps, beneath the luxury of orylag fur. There is also another bedroom, an office and a very beautiful bathroom on this floor. Although there is little natural light here, Stéphane hasn't tried to compensate with bright lights and pale colours. Instead, he has opted for a deep, womb-like red that's as dark and mysterious as the night.

Alleyways lead off the stunning Place aux Herbes in the small Roman town of Uzès in the Gard and meet up with a peripheral road. On a corner there stands a bank, an ordinary, functional bank just like any other, until you gaze upwards once inside while waiting for the next teller.

EASTERN PROMISE

Then you realize that you are standing under the most exquisite stone-constructed arch. This temple of commerce is built into what was an Ursuline convent in the early 18th century, but the real treasure of the building lies above – the extraordinary home created by Gérard and Danielle Labre. A discreet, rather ordinary door to the side of the bank's entrance gives no indication of what's to come.

Gérard has been an antiques dealer for 25 years, but before that he worked in catering and was a passionate collector, volunteering at the Guimet Museum in Paris and even lending some of his collected *objets* for exhibition. He eventually opened a shop in the city, but then moved south, as so many do, in search of a better life. He had a shop in Uzès for five years, but these days he sells from home, mainly to private clients by appointment only, and to museums all over the world.

RIGHT *The stone floor in the dining room was reclaimed from the Hôtel Particulier, in the centre of Uzès, when it was demolished. Two impressive cupboards, a 17th-century French fruitwood armoire on the left and, on the right, a 19th-century Indian example, with remnants of its original paint, are grand custodians of all the* appareil *for dining.*

Gérard is an expert in his field. He is often to be found with his nose deep in reference books, researching spiders, corals and fossils. One of his specialities is discovering rarities of such species and framing them, like floating amoebae, in seamless glass cases that are both ethereal and beautiful.

If you ever meet Gérard, make sure you allow plenty of time to talk to him. He is absolutely passionate about his chosen subjects and loves to share his knowledge, which he does in a most animated way. He is a privilege to know, and a rarity in a world that's generally more interested in the activities of the kind of business that operates beneath his home.

Gérard spends as many months as he can abroad. He's not just tracking down treasures – which he certainly does – but also running a Tibetan refugee charity. It is to Tibet that he and his wife eventually intend to retire. Retirement will not mean putting his feet up, however – a man with such vision will surely create something extraordinary and unique for his next home.

ABOVE LEFT *A tiny toy cockerel is unlikely to wake anyone from the dead.*
LEFT *Looking past the kitchen and through a low arch into the voluminous sitting room. Above the arch, Philippino crabs have been given the signature Labre glass-case treatment.*
OPPOSITE ABOVE *The thought of an acid-yellow and sage-green kitchen surely jars, but in this space it works very well.*
OPPOSITE BELOW *Fresh garlic bulbs bought from the weekly market.*

When Gérard and Danielle moved to Uzès from Paris in 2000, they took on an enormous project. The building, which had experienced various incarnations over the decades, was then a decaying and neglected theatre that had partially burned down. In one sense, their part of the building is still a theatre, showcasing Gérard's collections of Tibetan and Asian art – bizarre and rare objects in glass frames worthy of the Natural History Museum, religious iconography and lots of skulls; not in any way macabre, but more a representation of the transient nature of life as depicted in medieval vanitas paintings.

Behind the undistinguished front door, at the top of a narrow stone staircase and behind an orange velvet curtain, is a space that is truly humbling. Not wishing to aggrandize too much, for me this space has a wow factor comparable to that of the Egyptian

LEFT *An impressive 18th-century carved wooden figure of Vishnu, god of gods, preserver of the universe.*
BELOW CENTRE *Looking up at the 12-metre-high cupola from the living room.*
BELOW LEFT *Detail of the 18th-century staircase, made from stone quarried at the nearby Pont du Gard.*
RIGHT *A collection of 18th- and 19th-century tridents. These were originally carried on poles by Hindu holy men, or sadhus, on pilgrimage through India.*

pyramids. With its soaring stone cupola 12 metres high, constructed in the manner of Brunelleschi's 15th-century Duomo in Florence, this is certainly not your average living room. The three-piece suite comprises a Tibetan day bed and two prayer chairs, reminders of Gérard's passion for Tibet. Less esoteric is the huge flat-screen TV, but it's more likely to be showing a video of a choir of Tibetan monks, who have chanted in this very space, than an episode of the latest soap.

This impressive space leads into a kitchen that's on a more human scale, which, in turn, leads to a garden with a raised swimming pool. There's nothing unusual or privileged about having a pool in your garden when you live in the South of France… unless your garden and pool are on the first floor. It's an extraordinary achievement of engineering, and you can't

OPPOSITE *The ceiling-to-floor bespoke bookcases are filled with art and reference books — the font of the owners' encyclopaedic knowledge. An unusual 19th-century French oak library ladder also provides some extra shelf space.*

help wondering how they got a digger up the stairs, but, as the Egyptians proved, you can do amazing things without machinery. As you'd imagine, the garden is peaceful and meditative, with stunning views over the rooftops of the town.

The conversion of this building took more than two painstaking years to complete – a process that Gérard carefully documented with his camera.

Beyond the gargantuan living room, one continues up another staircase to the next level, home to the bedroom, bathroom, study/library and atelier. Like the kitchen, these rooms are all on a human scale and, with books everywhere, one feels secure and safe. It's a good job, though, that there are sturdy railings for those nervous of heights. The views from this floor are stunning. From a rooftop terrace off Danielle's studio, where she paints, one can look down, as if from the gods, through large glass doors into the cupola living room.

This remarkable home is not for the faint of heart. But it is an inspiration to anyone who likes the idea of living in a space that's very definitely 'outside the box'. If a triangular pyramid was good enough for the pharaohs, then a domed cupola is more than good enough for the Labres.

OPPOSITE *Danielle's atelier is a glass structure on the top floor, with panoramic views of the town of Uzès and the countryside beyond. What better place to be inspired?*
ABOVE *Danielle's collection of coral, lapis lazuli, glass and stone necklaces has been amassed during 25 years of travel. Too beautiful to be hidden in a jewel box, they are displayed on custom-made hooks.*
RIGHT *Art in progress and finished pieces by Danielle and others on the wall in various types of frame.*

The slightly battered Citroën DS, parked outside a stone house just west of Uzès, is the first sign that the owners have an interesting home. Behind the large gates, an explosion of fun and colour is affirmation indeed that here lives a really cool couple. No Renault Clio for them...

WHIMSICAL CHIC

Arnaud Serpollet and his artist wife, Valerie, have been antiques dealers for several years. They sell from La Chine Populaire, a large shared space in the centre of Uzès, and also from their home – a complicated, rambling house containing an overwhelming quantity of stock, largely dating from the 1950s and 1960s. Wandering through the labyrinth of cave-like rooms feels like a truly psychedelic experience. But don't be fooled. Arnaud's knowledge is extensive, and what appears chaotic is, in fact, carefully catalogued. When asked, he knows where everything is.

Music is a large part of Arnaud's life – in his spare time, he is a drummer and plays at local gigs. The record player is in constant use. Like all true music lovers, despite having piles of CDs, he still gets the greatest enjoyment from spinning vinyl. To an aficionado like Arnaud, the act of taking a record out of its sleeve, settling down with a cup of coffee or a glass of wine and reading the lyrics is pure joy. While listening to his music, Arnaud is to be found pottering around his balcony, tending his plants, tinkering beneath the bonnet of his beloved Citroën and fixing, restoring and preparing stock for the boutique.

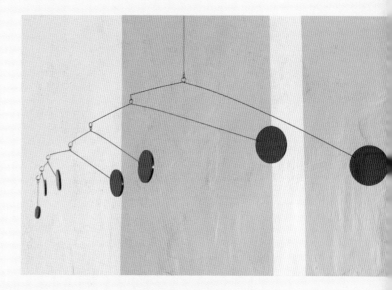

OPPOSITE *There is a brave but very successful contrast of materials and styles in the dining room. Around the traditional wooden French farmhouse table are four of Eero Saarinen's distinctive, plastic-coated aluminium Tulip chairs from the 1950s.* **ABOVE LEFT** *An exterior door in two colours is reminiscent of Peter Blake's 1960s abstract art.* **ABOVE RIGHT** *A simple Calderesque mobile constructed of wire and Perspex floats silently at the top of the stairs.*

ABOVE LEFT *At one time found in almost every French home, this coffee maker is an Italian style classic.* **LEFT** *Even the kitchen has not escaped Valerie's mosaics. Here, her work has extended to a bespoke splashback.* **ABOVE** *A Saarinen Tulip table and matching stools sit at a window of glass bricks in the guest living room.*

Valerie has her own studio in the building next door. She is a mosaic artist or, to use the correct term, practises the art of *la picassiette*. She collects old plates – plain, flowered or patterned, chipped or cracked, it matters not – which she then breaks into small pieces, carefully files into different shapes and sizes, and sticks onto pots, vases, plaques or anything else that appeals. Her source of inspiration is Raymond Isidore, who, between 1938 and 1964, took the art to the extreme, covering his whole house in Chartres, including the furniture, with broken china.

THIS PAGE *Piles of plates found at* brocantes *and* déballages *await Valerie's hammer. The planters against the wall are examples of her work. The bunch of 1950s belles look on smilingly.*

ABOVE *Jaunty 1950s birdcages hang in a row on a wire inside the entrance gates. Little plastic birds complete the farce.* **BELOW LEFT** *In the pink room, where Arnaud keeps his tools of the trade, on top of a green painted cupboard full of more glass and ceramics is a collection of 1940s French green glazed pots.* **BELOW RIGHT** *Yet another Saarinen Tulip base, this time married to a 1970s leather seat. The sunlight shines through two pieces of an enormous collection of studio glass, throwing a crimson shadow on the 1950s coffee table.*

RIGHT *The decoratively carved oak chair c. 1900, a copy of something made much earlier, is the only seating in the library. Shelves are packed with paperbacks and reference books, interspersed with the odd piece of studio pottery.*

Arnaud, who was born in Paris, moved to this remote country village with his family as a child and still lives in the same house. Like so many ancient stone village houses, the house conforms to no architectural principle – it feels as if a fairy simply waved her magic wand and it all appeared in a puff of smoke. You can wander here and there, never quite sure of which terrace you will end up on, but that doesn't really matter (unless you're in a rush to find the bathroom).

Going through a door to the right of the main gates, you climb a steep and uneven stone staircase with no handrail. Floating at the top of the stairs is a Calderesque mobile with transparent red Perspex discs, which signals the beginning of a kaleidoscopic adventure. Across the ceiling, all the way down the opposite wall and back again, Arnaud has beautifully painted in acid-yellow paint a very long and fat tubular 'U' shape. It's a bold statement that may sound odd, but is, in fact, artful and considered, setting the stage perfectly for the retro furniture and brightly coloured ornaments.

The room of entry is the main family room, a generous space for living and dining, with a small corner housing the retro kitchen. A balcony runs the entire length of the room and is accessed by a pair of double doors behind the dining table. These are always kept open – even in winter, South-of-France skies are often sunny and bright blue. In front of a large, traditional fireplace where logs burn in winter sits a wide, low 1960s sofa with bright purple cushions. Any preconceptions of quaint rural France are thrown out of the window in this home.

Off the kitchen, a winding corridor, lined with shelves showcasing French studio pottery and Danish Holmegaard glass, leads you to a tiny room – a library with floor-to-ceiling shelves full with reference books on the many diverse subjects that interest Arnaud and Valerie, as well as an abundance of French paperback novels, many of them bound in white, and lots of Asterix books. This room has a slim, arched window with a view over the rooftops of the village. With the doors closed, you feel as if you're in a monk's cell. It would be easy to spend peaceful days of solitude here, lost in the books of Camus or Sartre.

Pass through another section of corridor, cross a terrace, climb some more stairs and you finally end up at the couple's bedroom. This, too, is lined with more pottery and books.

A creeper-covered balcony looks down onto the courtyard with its big gates. Here, Arnaud has garlanded a tree with strands of multicoloured plastic beads and butterflies. Such joy, such whimsy, and so unusual in our conventional world, where so many aspire to hedges of neatly trimmed privet. This family are living their dream and are fortunate to make an honest living from it.

BELOW LEFT *On the inside of the gates, among an array of advertising plaques and enamel plates, is the eponymous Red Cow, laughing at scantily clad ladies serving pastis and motor oil.* **BELOW RIGHT** *More enamel advertising signs on a terrace. It is said that there are 40 shades of green and this metal chair and window frame represent just two. Although at opposite ends of the chart, the colours do not jar.*

TOP AND ABOVE *A collection of 1960s model cars, some of them fresh from the factory on the Dinky transporter at the back. Not satisfied with his model collection, Arnaud also has the real thing — a dashing black and orange 1950s Citroën DS. Though far from being in concourse condition, unlike his model cars it is in daily use.* **RIGHT** *The model cars shown above are parked among a collection of studio pottery and plates on glass and wooden shelves in the bedroom.*

TREASURE TROVE

Although typically French from the outside, Mary Champ's house does have a touch of the Irish homeland about it, for Mary (then Lynch) was born in West Cork. Stone-built over two centuries from 1700, it is a partially restored rambling *mas*, typical of the Languedoc-Roussillon region. There is also a barn and three gardens, two of which are separated from the house by a tiny road used only by the neigbours. Entry is no longer through the huge and permanently chained gates at the front of the house, but via a red wooden door secreted around the corner.

Mary was an antiques dealer for many years, first in London, then Barcelona. Although she's not actually trading at the moment, once a dealer, always a dealer. She never misses the weekly Sunday market in Uzès, held

ABOVE *A collection of jugs, all made from pewter, has a medieval quality.* **RIGHT** *In the attic, a 19th-century French chaise longue, with remnants of fringing, has the air of a colourful Miss Havisham. Renovated and reupholstered, this dilapidated treasure would become a very commercial piece, but the romance of it would be lost forever.*

The Champ house is a busy one — there's Mary, her gorgeous twin daughters Beatrice and Florence, no fewer than nine cats and four dogs, and a constant stream of visitors. Mary has lived in her house, set in a beautiful, elevated village 10km west of Uzès, for the past ten years.

THIS PAGE *Draped in an antique linen sheet, the circular kitchen table overlooks the terrace and garden. The unusual wonky pewter plate looks like a preacher's hat.*

ABOVE *The unusual shade of green on the walls was a homemade mix, as was the dye used on the antique linen sheets. These conceal shelves crammed with tweed blankets, quilts, monogrammed linens and antique tickings. The table and chair are 19th-century English oak.* **RIGHT** *Antique lace gives a softer look than curtains in the study. The armchair, draped in vibrant red ticking, fills the window space.*

at the rugby club, and can be spotted without fail carrying away armfuls of ubiquitous French monogrammed linen sheets or yet another pewter candlestick.

Mary's home is rustic and eclectic, but above all unique, conforming to no particular style, except her own. She has no time for the grey and taupe minimalist brigade. The house is crammed with colourful textiles and vintage clothes, hinting at Mary's passion for fabrics and her much-admired eccentric chic.

Passing through the red door into the main salon, you're immediately struck by the soaring, beamed ceiling. This room is impressive. It's divided roughly into a large seating area in front of a huge stone fireplace on the left with two squashy sofas, six large armchairs and an imposing, wall-length Cevenol fruitwood buffet. Every one of the chairs is covered or draped in a different fabric, according to whatever has been the latest Sunday market find. The walls are painted with *chaux* (limewash) tinted yellow, while the interior doors are the same red as the entrance.

The right-hand side of this barn-like space has a dining table, but it's more usually laid out with dress patterns and a sewing machine than formal dinner place settings. Meals in winter are always taken in the large, homely kitchen with its terracotta floor tiles. The room opens out onto a large terrace, where everyone, including the dogs, eats in the summer. The pink walls pick out the natural hue of the ancient terracotta roof tiles, a feature of all the houses in the hamlet. The kitchen walls are covered in paintings – finds from art fairs in England, France and Spain, gifts and the girls' own work. Some are framed, some are not. As in all good Irish Catholic homes, the inevitable sacred heart presides over all.

Typical of many French houses, rooms lead on from one another. The room off the kitchen has the feel of a Vermeer interior. The floor tiles are particularly beautiful, and the home-blended hues of the walls and drapes are unique – there are no dye or paint charts! Essentially a large cupboard, this room is storage for sheets, napkins and bedspreads – further proof, if it were needed, of Mary's lifelong magpie instinct for picking up exquisite textiles and fragments. Each ample shelf is filled to capacity with neatly folded treasures.

Next is the main bathroom, another large space with a freestanding bath and yet more rails of vintage dresses, racks of jumpers and baskets of scarves – a girls' paradise. The bathroom follows through to three consecutive bedrooms. The large master bedroom is painted a restful blue – a favourite shade of Mary's. The bed is covered with a vintage French patchwork quilt and,

OPPOSITE ABOVE *Blue floral curtains made from antique mattress covering are used to conceal kitchen paraphernalia.*
OPPOSITE BELOW *The unused fireplace is now the felines' feeding hole.*
RIGHT *This old work bench has been given a new lease of life as a console in the hallway. Flanked by a pair of pewter candlesticks, the large mirror exudes charm. The painting is by Florence.*
BELOW *The glazed tiles in the bathroom are Moroccan. An antique sink reveals the not-unattractive puzzle of plumbing beneath.*

OPPOSITE *This 19th-century French gilt mirror leaning against the wall of the main salon has beautifully foxed mercury glass. There is an abstract quality about the reflected striped kilim used as a tablecloth, while the half-dressed mannequin is just surreal!* **BELOW** *An old fruit-picking ladder is a quirky way to display a girl's favourite high heels.* **RIGHT AND FAR RIGHT** *An armless doll, a sailor boy and a blind bear are part of a large collection of well-loved vintage toys.* **BELOW RIGHT** *Another collection of colourful quilts and bedspreads.* **BOTTOM RIGHT** *Never seen out in the midday sun without a wide-brimmed hat, Mary displays her extensive collection of* chapeaux *in the bedroom.*

at any given time, at least a cat or two. A picture of the Virgin Mary on the wall gazes down upon it all with a serene smile.

The final room on this floor is a second, smaller salon, where a simple, rustic bookshelf takes up one whole wall. Made from huge slabs of rough-hewn and unpainted wood, reminiscent of railway sleepers, they creak under the weight of books in Gaelic, English, French and Spanish, and back issues of well-thumbed magazines.

Comfortable and lived-in, Mary's home is inspirational, especially for her two daughters growing up in this rural part of France. There are fashion and interiors magazines dotted around the house, so they know who's wearing what in Milan and Paris, and what the latest interiors trend is in London or New York. Having a mother as creative as Mary, it comes as no surprise that the daughters have developed their own very individual styles and promise to be hugely successful in their chosen careers: Beatrice in fashion, Florence as a painter.

RIGHT *Rusty green gates lead to the pool opposite the house.*
OPPOSITE *The powdery soft blue of the exterior paintwork soon fades and cracks in the heat of summer. More decorative than practical, these 19th-century iron and woven metal mesh loungers on the main terrace have seen better days.*

The girls each have their own large studio space in the attic, where, if they leave the windows open at night, the bats come in to roost. Here, you'll find an unrestored chaise longue, a tailor's dummy with a couture creation made from cardboard tubing, empty picture frames and slabs of white marble awaiting the perfect table base.

Antiques dealers of the world are united in their belief that nothing need ever be thrown away. Who needs to buy new when everything old has a far more interesting tale to tell? Besides, it's much more fun hunting and bargaining than picking up one of many identical pieces from a shelf and queuing at the checkout. One thing is sure: if Mary reopens those vast gates for business, there will be some very happy customers.

SOURCE DIRECTORY

UK SOURCES

ANTIQUES

JOSEPHINE RYAN ANTIQUES
josephineryanantiques.
myshopify.com
*Chandeliers, antique mirrors,
furniture and accessories.*

APPLEY HOARE
appleyhoare.com
*Rare and unusual French
country antiques.*

THE FRENCH HOUSE
thefrenchhouse.co.uk
*French antiques, fabrics and china.
Showrooms in both London and
York — visit the website for details.*

KATHARINE POLE
+44 (0)20 7286 5630
katharinepole.com
French antique textiles.

LA MAISON
+44 (0)20 7729 9646
lamaisonlondon.com
*Antique and reproduction
furniture, mirrors and lighting.*

MAISON ARTEFACT
273 Lillie Road
London SW6 7LL
+44 (0)20 7381 2500
maisonartefact.com
*French, Swedish and some English
antiques and garden statuary.*

RELIC ANTIQUES
127 Pancras Road
London NW1 1UN
+44 (0)20 7485 7810
rubylane.com/shop/relic
*Country furniture, folk art and
fairground art and antiques.*

ROBERT YOUNG ANTIQUES
68 Battersea Bridge Road
London SW11 3AG
+44 (0)20 7228 7847
robertyoungantiques.com
Country antiques and folk art.

SPENCER SWAFFER ANTIQUES
30 High Street
Arundel
West Sussex BN18 9AB
+44 (0)1903 882132
spencerswaffer.com
Decorative French antiques.

SALVAGE & RECLAMATION

**ANDY THORNTON
ARCHITECTURAL ANTIQUES**
Victoria Mills
Stainland Road
Greetland
Halifax
West Yorkshire HX4 8AD
+44 (0)1422 377314
andythornton.com
*Architectural antiques, architectural
salvage and quirky vintage pieces.*

LASSCO
30 Wandsworth Road,
London SW8 2LG
+44 (0)20 7394 2100
lassco.co.uk
*Salvaged floors, doors, mantelpieces,
sanitaryware and much more.*

TEXTILES & WALLPAPERS

CABBAGES AND ROSES
23 Sydney Street
London SW3 6NR
+44 (0)20 7352 7333
cabbagesandroses.com
Romantic wallpapers and fabrics.

COLE & SON
cole-and-son.com
Fine printed wallpapers.

PEONY & SAGE
peonyandsage.com
*French-inspired bed linen,
wallpaper, fabrics and accessories.*

WHALEYS (BRADFORD) LTD
+44 (0)1274 576718
whaleys-bradford.ltd.uk
*Utility fabrics — jute, linen,
canvas and raw silks.*

PAINTS & TILES

FARROW & BALL
farrow-ball.com
Paint in subtle, muted shades.

LIMESTONE GALLERY
limestonegallery.com
*Limestone flooring and
handmade French tiles.*

PAINT & PAPER LIBRARY
3 Elystan Street
London SW3 3NT
+44 (0)20 7823 7755
paint-paper.co.uk
*Subtle, beautiful paint
and wallpapers.*

**PAPERS AND PAINTS
BY PATRICK BATY**
4 Park Walk
London SW10 0AD
+44 (0)20 7352 8626
papersandpaints.co.uk
*Historical paint colours and
colour consultancy.*

KITCHENS

ASTIER DE VILLATTE
astierdevillatte.com
Elegant and simple faïence china.

LA MAISON BLEUE
lamaisonbleue.co.uk
French table and kitchen accessories.

FOURNEAUX DE FRANCE
+44 (0)1202 733011
lacanche.co.uk
*Makers of Lacanche
range-style cookers.*

BATHROOMS

CATCHPOLE & RYE
Chelsea Walk
282-284 Fulham Road
London SW10 9EW
+44 (0)1233 840840
www.catchpoleandrye.com
*Antique and reproduction
sanitaryware.*

STIFFKEY BATHROOMS
89 Upper St Giles Street
Norwich
Norfolk NR2 1AB
+44 (0)1603 627850
stiffkeybathrooms.com
Antique sanitaryware.

LIGHTING

DAVID CANEPA LIGHTING
canepalighting.co.uk
Wall lights and chandeliers.

MIRRORS

JASPER JACKS
jasperjacks.com
*Large stock of antique French mirrors,
lighting and other decorative items.*

GARDEN FURNITURE & ORNAMENTS

JANE WALTON
janewalton.co.uk
*Antique garden ornaments,
furniture and decorative items.*

JARDINIQUE
Old Park Farm
Abbey Road
Alton
Hampshire GU34 4AP
+44 (0)1420 560055
jardinique.co.uk
*Antiques and antique
garden ornaments.*

US SOURCES

ANTIQUES

ELIZABETH STREET GALLERY
209 Elizabeth Street
New York, NY 10012
+1 212 941 4800
elizabethstreetgallery.com
Architectural and garden antiques.

ERON JOHNSON ANTIQUES
389 South Lipan Street
Denver, CO 80223
+1 303 777 8700
eronjohnsonantiques.com
Online retailer of fine antiques.

SALVAGE &
RECLAMATION

ARCHITECTURAL ACCENTS
2711 Piedmont Road NE
Atlanta, GA 30305
+1 404 266 8700
architecturalaccents.com
*Antique fixtures, architectural
antiques and high-quality
reproductions.*

CARAVATI'S INC.
104 East Second Street
Richmond, VA 23224
+1 804 232 4175
caravatis.com
Architectural salvage.

TEXTILES &
WALLPAPERS

GRACIOUS HOME
gracioushome.com
Bedding, linens and accessories.

**RACHEL ASHWELL
SHABBY CHIC**
shabbychic.com
*French-inspired vintage-style
monogrammed linens and bedding
plus furniture and lighting.*

SCALAMANDRE SILK, INC.
979 Third Avenue
New York, NY 10022
+1 212 980 3888
scalamandre.com
Reproductions of classic fabrics.

THIBAUT
+1 800 223 0704
thibautdesign.com
Textiles and wallpaper.

PAINTS & TILE

COUNTRY FLOORS
15 East Sixteenth Street
New York, NY 10003
+1 212 627 8300
countryfloors.com
*Ceramics, natural stone
and terracotta.*

FINE PAINTS OF EUROPE
+1 800 332 1556
finepaintsofeurope.com
*Fine quality imported Dutch
paints, including ECO waterbased
paints and traditional oil paint.*

**OLD FASHIONED MILK
PAINT COMPANY**
+1 978 448 6336
milkpaint.com
*Historic ecologically friendly paints
made from natural pigments.*

KITCHENS &
BATHROOMS

**HOUSE OF ANTIQUE
HARDWARE**
houseofantiquehardware.com
*Vintage-style plumbing fixtures
and plumbing parts including faucets
and bathroom accessories.*

**THE PERIOD BATH
SUPPLY COMPANY**
periodbath.com
*Fine reproduction clawfoot bathtubs,
faucets and showers as well as some
salvaged original pieces.*

RESTORATION HARDWARE
restorationhardware.com
*Fine hardware, home furnishings,
lighting and other accessories.*

LIGHTING

ANN MORRIS ANTIQUES
239 East Sixtieth Street
New York, NY 10022
+1 212 755 3308
annmorrislighting.com
Reproduction lamps and shades.

GARDEN FURNITURE
& ORNAMENTS

DETROIT GARDEN WORKS
1794 Pontiac Drive
Sylvan Lake, MI 48320
+1 248 335 8089
detroitgardenworks.com
French and English garden antiques.

FAIRS & MARKETS

UK

ADAM'S ANTIQUES FAIRS
adamsantiquesfairs.com
Antique and vintage fashion fairs.

**DECORATIVE ANTIQUES
AND TEXTILES FAIR**
Battersea Park, London
decorativefair.com
*Three fairs a year, offering high-
quality, competitively priced antiques
and 20th-century design.*

**INTERNATIONAL ANTIQUES
AND COLLECTORS FAIRS**
iacf.co.uk
*Antiques fairs held at Shepton Mallet,
Ardingly, Newark and Newbury.*

FRANCE
L'ISLE SUR LA SORGUE
*A historic town in the southern Rhône
valley famous for its antique shops.
Open weekends and holidays, from
10am–7pm.*

**MARCHÉ AUX PUCES DE
ST OUEN**
Porte de Clignancourt, Paris
*One of the largest antiques markets
in the world. Open Saturdays
9.30am–6pm.*

USA
BRIMFIELD ANTIQUE SHOW
Route 20
Brimfield, MA 01010
brimfieldshow.com
*This famous flea market runs for
a week in May, July and September.*

**HELL'S KITCHEN
FLEA MARKET**
West 39th Street at 9th Avenue
New York, NY
+1 212-220-0239
hellskitchenfleamarket.com
Weekends 9am–5pm.

GEORGETOWN FLEA MARKET
1819 35th St NW
Washington, DC 20007
+1 202 775 FLEA
www.georgetownfleamarket.com
Sundays 8am–6pm.

BUSINESS CREDITS

JOSEPHINE RYAN
E: jryanantiques@aol.com
www.josephineryanantiques.
co.uk
*Josephine's French home is available
to rent at:*
www.josephineryanfrance.
co.uk

MAISON ARTEFACT
273 Lillie Road
London SW6 7LL.
T: +44 (0)20 7381 2500
www.maisonartefact.com

**STÉPHANE BROUTIN
ANTIQUITÉS DÉCORATION**
Passage du Pont
(L'Isle aux Brocantes)
7 Avenue des quatre Otages
84800 L'Isle sur la Sorgue
France
T: +33 (0)4 90 38 27 79
M: +33 (0)6 03 22 97 97
E: broutin.s@wanadoo.fr

CHÂTEAU DE CHRISTIN
M: +33 (0)6 12 36 13 09
Contact Olivier and Nina
Delafargue
www.chateaudechristin.fr
E: chateaudechristin@orange.fr

**JEAN-LOUIS FAGES
ANTIQUITÉS – DÉCORATION
(NÎMES) SARL INTERIEUR
GANACHE**
3 Place du Marché
30000 Nîmes
T: +33 (0)4 66 27 38 23
E: Mataoll@hotmail.fr

GALERIE ET CAETERA
40 rue de Poitou
75003 Paris
E: franckdelmarcelle@yahoo.fr
www.franckdelmarcelle.com

B&B available at:
www.maisonmistre.fr

APPLEY HOARE ANTIQUES
22 Pimlico Road
London SW1W 8LJ
T: +44 (0)20 7730 7070
E: appley@appleyhoare.com
www.appleyhoare.com

GÉRARD LABRE
2 Boulevard des Alliés
30700 Uzès
France
T: +33 (0)6 20 69 70 32
+33 (0)4 66 37 62 15
E: glabre@orange.fr

STÉPHANE OLIVIER
3 rue de l'Université
75007 Paris
T: +33 (0)1 42 96 10 00
E: rivegauche@stephaneolivier.fr

and

LA PETITE MAISON
10 rue Paul Bert
93400 St Ouen
France
T: +33 (0)1 40 10 56 69

THIBAULT NOSSEREAU
Marché Paul Bert
Alleé 3, Stand 159
Rue des Rosiers
93400 Saint Ouen
France
T: +33 (0)6 08 64 09 19

SPENCER SWAFFER ANTIQUES
30 High Street
Arundel
West Sussex BN18 9AB
T: +44 (0)1903 882132
www.spencerswaffer.com

ARNAUD AND VALERIE
SERPOLLET
Le Chine Populaire
7 avenue Libération
30700 Uzès
France
T: +33 4 66 03 34 83

MAXIME AND BERNARD
CASSAGNES
La Fabrique
11390 Brousses
France
T: +33 4 68 26 57 55
(by appointment only)

PICTURE CREDITS

Front cover: Appley Hoare's 18th-century converted Eau-de-Vie factory in the South of France (appleyhoare.com); Endpapers: Appley Hoare's 18th-century converted Eau-de-Vie factory in the South of France; Pages 1–3 Josephine Ryan Antiques; 4 Château de Christin, Chambres d'Hôtes de Luxe, Reception – Seminaires; 5 above left Appley Hoare's 18th-century converted Eau-de-Vie factory in the South of France; 5 above right The London home of Shane Meredith and Victoria Davar of Maison Artefact; 5 below left The home of Spencer and Freya Swaffer in Arundel; 7 above left www.franckdelmarcelle.com; 7 above centre The London home of Shane Meredith and Victoria Davar of Maison Artefact; 7 above right and centre left Appley Hoare's 18th-century converted Eau-de-Vie factory in the South of France; 7 centre The home of Bernard and Maxime Cassagnes in France; 7 centre right The home of Spencer and Freya Swaffer in Arundel; 7 below left Appley Hoare's 18th-century converted Eau-de-Vie factory in the South of France; 7 below centre The home of Mary Champ in France; 7 below right Stéphane Olivier; 8 above left and below left Stéphane Olivier's home in Paris; 8 above centre and below right Château de Christin, Chambres d'Hôtes de Luxe, Reception – Seminaires; 8 above right The home of Mary Champ in France; 8 below centre www.franckdelmarcelle.com; 9 above left and centre Appley Hoare's 18th-century converted Eau-de-Vie factory in the South of France; 9 above right and below left The home of Jean-Louis Fages and Matthieu Ober in Nîmes; 9 below left www.franckdelmarcelle.com; 9 below centre The home of Spencer and Freya Swaffer in Arundel; 10–11 Appley Hoare's 18th-century converted Eau-de-Vie factory in the South of France; 12–23 Josephine Ryan Antiques; 24–35 Appley Hoare's 18th-century converted Eau-de-Vie factory in the South of France; 36–45 The London home of Shane Meredith and Victoria Davar of Maison Artefact; 46–55 Stéphane Broutin Antiquités Décoration; 56–67 Château de Christin, Chambres d'Hôtes de Luxe, Reception–Seminaires; 68–75 The home of Jean-Louis Fages and Matthieu Ober in Nîmes; 76–85 www.franckdelmarcelle.com; 86–95 The home of Spencer and Freya Swaffer in Arundel; 96–107 The home of Christine and Denis Nossereau in L'Isle sur la Sorgue; 108–109 Stéphane Olivier's home in Paris; 110–119 The home of Bernard and Maxime Cassagnes in France; 120–127 Stéphane Olivier's home in Paris; 128–135 Gérard and Danièlle Labre's home near Uzès in France; 136–143 The home of Arnaud and Valerie Serpollet near Sainte Chaptes; 144–153 The home of Mary Champ in France; 155 The London home of Shane Meredith and Victoria Davar of Maison Artefact; 156 The home of Bernard and Maxime Cassagnes in France; Back cover: The home of Spencer and Freya Swaffer in Arundel.

INDEX

ACKNOWLEDGMENTS

The need to be creative is my *raison d'etre* and, in rising to the challenge of writing this book, I have discovered another means of expressing myself – one that has proved surprisingly satisfying. I have my son Cahal to both blame and thank for daring me to write this book!

A year in the making – from plotting and planning, to photography, to dotting the i's – and it has been a passionate time. There have been days of sunny photo shoots and long nights spent writing at the kitchen table and learning new skills, but it has also been a traumatic time in my life that has forged great change. I need to express my gratitude to a few very special people – Matthew and Taina, Judith and Ian, Colette and Gosia – without whose unstinting love and support this book could not have happened.

To all my fellow dealers and the other contributors, thank you for having such good taste, for creating homes worth photographing, and for serving delicious lunches! In particular, thanks to Vicky Davar, who has been a superstar friend and well deserves her front-cover fame. Thanks also to the team at RPS, especially Alison Starling and Jess Walton, whose patience and understanding was over and above the call of duty.

Helen Ridge deserves a medal for all her help with the text. Thanks to two fabulous and creative 'sisters' – Claire Richardson and her assistant Ellie Laycock – for taking and producing their usual high standard of beautiful photos and, perhaps more importantly, for being great fun. Thank you Paul Ryan – not for moving to Australia, but for being the one who always picks up the phone to see what his big sis is up to, and being proud and encouraging.

Last but by no means least, I shout out thanks to my little family: Cahal and Uma Rose, two unique and very special children whom I adore, and to Mohit Bakaya for giving them to me and for being my long-suffering partner and husband for 18 years, and hopefully my friend forever.

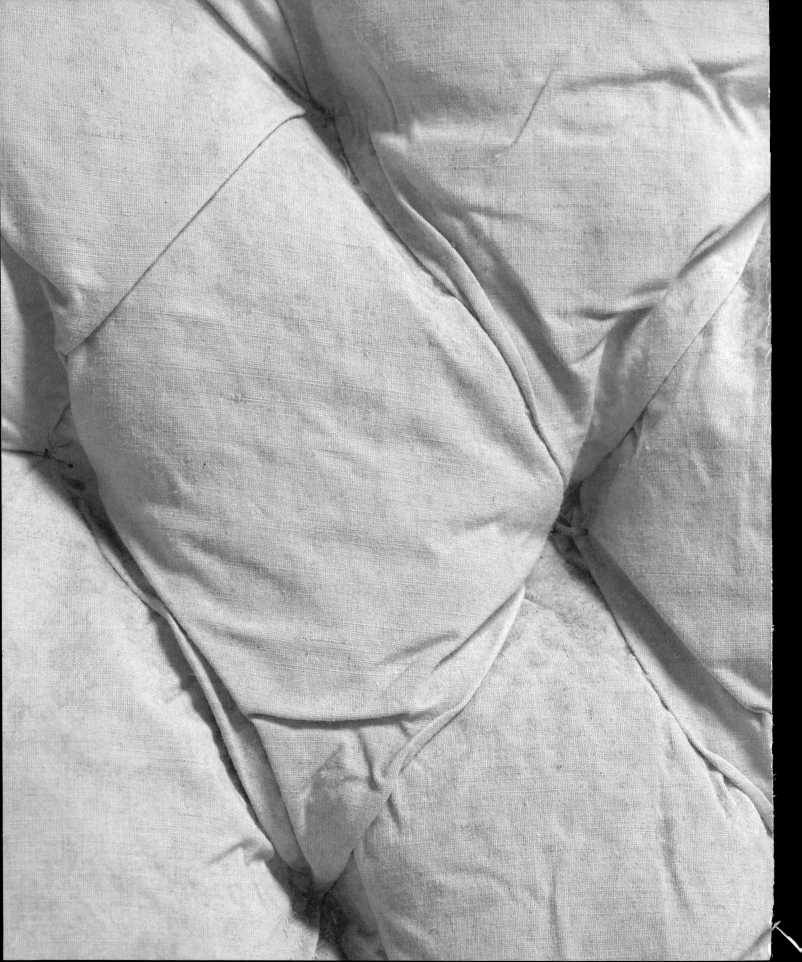